Fresh
·F·I·S·H·
COOKBOOK

Fresh
·F·I·S·H·
COOKBOOK

WHSMITH

EXCLUSIVE
·BOOKS·

Acknowledgments
The publishers would like to thank
the Sea Fish Industry Authority for
supplying the colour photographs
reproduced on pages 25, 33, 37, 45, 49,
61, 69, 73, 77, 81, 85, 89 and 92.

© Ward Lock Limited 1987
Produced specially for W. H. Smith & Sons
by Ward Lock Limited, 8 Clifford Street
London W1X 1RB, an Egmont Company

Text filmset in $10\frac{1}{2}$ on $11\frac{1}{2}$ point Goudy Old Style
by Advanced Filmsetters (Glasgow) Ltd

Edited by Pam Cary

Printed and bound in Spain
by Graficromo S.A., Cordoba

ISBN 0 7063 6617 4

CONTENTS

INTRODUCTION

The huge variety of fish that is so accessible in every shape and form makes fish one of the most versatile foods to cook with. Yet it is also one of the most underestimated. In the past, when fish was compulsory eating on Fridays and Saturdays, it developed a reputation for being bland, tasteless, unappetizing, rather boring and generally much too difficult to bother with.

Now, with good fishmongers being easy to find and supermarkets introducing their own appealing fresh fish and shell fish counters, it is time to shake off this outdated stigma and allow such a versatile and nutritionally spectacular food to become a regular feature in our kitchens.

This cookbook offers substantial and wholesome meals for the family, appetizing and adventurous teas and suppers, exciting dinner ideas for guests, successful party appetizers; and most important of all, attractive and economical recipes for the cook.

With up to sixty different varieties to choose from, fish is as near perfect a food nutritionally as we are likely to find. Low in calories and carbohydrates yet high in protein, B vitamins and essential minerals, fish is the number one choice for good eating and good all-round health.

Notes

It is important to follow either the metric or the Imperial measures when using the recipes in this book. All measurements are given in both *except* spoon measures, when only the Imperial spoon measurements are given. Use the following standard conversion:

1.5 ml spoon/$\frac{1}{4}$ teaspoon
2.5 ml spoon/$\frac{1}{2}$ teaspoon
5 ml spoon/1 teaspoon
10 ml spoon/2 teaspoons
15 ml spoon/1 tablespoon or 3 teaspoons
30 ml spoon/2 tablespoons

All spoon measures are level.
Where tinned foods are used, the undrained weight is given.
When flour is called for, use plain flour unless otherwise stated.

ABOUT FISH

Choosing fresh fish

Unprocessed fish straight from the sea, river or fish farm is referred to as *wet fish*. It should be really fresh and should be cooked the day that it is bought. One reason why fish is unpopular with some people could be the fear that it has 'gone off'. The texture and flavour of fish which is a few days old is quite different from the succulent feel and fine flavour of really fresh fish.

With modern methods of transportation, fish on the inland fishmonger's slab should be almost as fresh as that sold at the seaside and it is certainly not in the fishmonger's interests to sell stale fish. However, if you are not sure of your fishmonger, your eyes and nose can provide you with all the information you need.

Here are the points to look for:

- The fish should have a fresh saline smell, not too fishy nor smelling of ammonia

- The flesh should be firm and springy to the touch. Avoid fish with droopy tails. Test the flesh with your fingers. If an imprint remains after the fish has been handled, the fish is not fresh

- Choose fish that are bright in colour—all fish loses its brilliancy with age. Look at the dark side of flat fish, for this side shows age first: instead of being bright and shiny it becomes dull

- The eyes should be bright and bulging. Avoid fish with dull and sunken eyes

- The gills of most fish should be red

- For smoked fish, check that the skin is dry and has a bright and healthy bloom. Avoid fish whose skin is damp or slimy

- When buying fillets or steaks look for firm, translucent flesh and avoid any that have a yellowish tinge to them

Storing fish

Once wet fish has been bought it should be used as quickly as possible. If, however, it has to be stored overnight, it should be cleaned, washed and dried and placed in a covered container in the refrigerator. Never leave fish in its original wrappings and always make sure that is well covered or the smell will pervade everything else that is stored in the refrigerator. A good place to store fish is in the tray immediately below the ice-making compartment. If you are not sure of the freshness of the fish, sprinkle with a little salt or lemon juice.

Commercially frozen fish should be taken home as quickly as possible after purchase and placed in the freezer where it will keep for up to three months. In the ice-making compartments of star-marked refrigerators the storage times are:- *—1 week: **—1 month: ***—3 months.

If the fish starts to defrost on the way home, remove the fish from its wrappings and use as wet fish. Never attempt to refreeze fish that has thawed.

Frozen fish is best thawed in the refrigerator but it can be thawed at room temperature if it is to be used at once. Keep the drip from the thawing fish for soups and sauces. Never thaw fish in water as this results in the loss of valuable nutrients.

Smoked and salted fish should be kept in the refrigerator and used within two or three days. Pickled and canned fish will keep until the container is opened, after which it should be eaten as soon as possible. Canned fish has a shelf life of about two years if it is packed in sauce and five years if packed in oil.

Preparing fish

Except for small round fish, most fish caught by commercial fishermen are gutted at sea. Only fish such as herrings, mackerel, and red mullet have to be gutted by the fishmonger or in the kitchen.

Scaling

If the scales are thick and coarse and need to be taken off, eg from sea bream, herring, or red mullet, this job must be done first. Lay the fish on soft kitchen paper to make cleaning up easier. With sharp scissors, cut off the fins; then, holding the tail, scrape both sides of the fish towards the head with the back of the knife. Rinse occasionally to remove the loose scales.

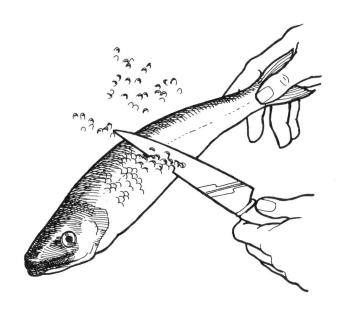

Cleaning

Some small fish, like fresh sardines and whitebait, are cooked and served complete, but most have to be gutted. This simply means making a cut in the right place, removing the intestines and cleaning the cavity of blood, membrane, and black skin. At some seasons, the roe takes up a lot of the cavity space, and both hard and soft roes should be kept as they make good eating. After cleaning, lightly rinse the cut area with cold water and pat dry.

Flat fish: Place the fish, dark skin up, on soft kitchen paper and locate the gill cover, positioned just behind the head. Make a deep cut from the centre line of the fish out to the fin just at the rear of the gill opening. Remove the intestines, but if the fish is to be cooked whole, leave the roe in place. To complete the cleaning, trim the 'frill' fins and tail back to the body. You can cut off the heads of plaice and lemon sole, but the head of a Dover sole is normally left on.

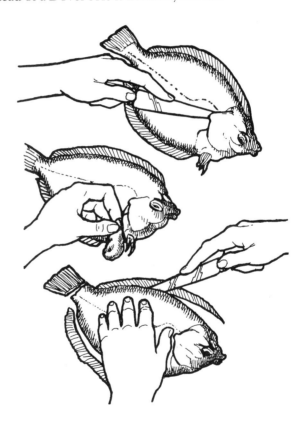

Large round fish: Cut the belly lengthways, from the gills to a point about two-thirds the length of the fish from the head. Remove the entrails, saving the roe if required, rinse thoroughly, and pat dry.

Small round fish: Clean most white fish and trout as described above. It is usual to remove mackerel heads before preparing, which makes cleaning easier. Herring are different because the entrails to be disposed of are minimal. Just make a downward cut behind the gills and pull the head back; then clean the area before rinsing. Leave the roe in place if grilling or cooking whole.

Skinning

Removing the skin from a slippery fish can be tricky and it may be simpler to cook the fish first. Dover soles should have at least the dark skin removed because it is coarser than that of lemon sole or plaice.

Flat fish: Lay the fish on a wooden board, white side down. With a sharp knife or scissors cut the 'frill' fins and tail back to the fish, if not already done, and scrape the tail end until the skin starts to lift. It is then easy to free a piece of skin; now slip the thumb or the end of a round-bladed knife under it and loosen the skin from the flesh, working towards the heads. When enough has been loosened like this, pull it off from the tail to head end. Repeat the process on the white side if required.

Work cautiously on soft-skinned fish, so as not to tear the flesh.

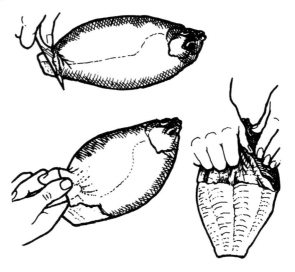

Round fish: Remove all the fins and make a cut in the skin all around the fish behind the head. It also helps to make a thin cut along the backbone of the fish. Starting on one side, loosen the skin from the belly flap and gradually pull towards the tail. Take care not to remove the flesh at the same time. It may help to hold the flesh down with the flat of a knife blade, and to dip your fingers in dry salt to give a firmer grip. Then skin the other side of the fish.

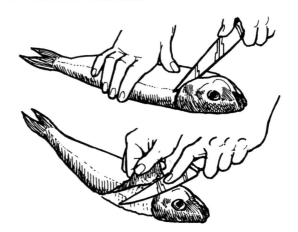

Filleting

Filleting means removing the flesh in two or four whole slices from the head and central bone structure. The head, bones, and skin of white fish are the basis for natural fish stock and should not be thrown away. If the fishmonger is filleting the fish, always ask him for the bones and trimmings to use for stock.

Flat fish: Lay the fish on a flat surface with its tail towards you. With a sharp, pointed knife, make a cut down the centre of the back right down to the backbone, from just behind the head to the tail. Then, turning the knife so that it lies flat against the bones, cut the flesh free from the bone, using the bone structure as a guide. Cut and loosen the fillet all the way to the edge of the fish and lift free.

Repeat the process with the other top fillet; then turn the fish over, and remove the two fillets from the other side in the same way.

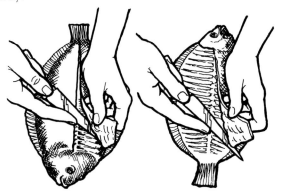

Round fish: Lay the gutted fish on its side and cut round behind the head. Then insert the point of the knife into the back of the fish, just behind the head, and cut right down the backbone all the way to the tail. Keeping the knife flat, and pressed against the rib bones, slice the fillet free along the length of the fish. Turn the fish over and remove the second fillet in the same fashion. Rinse, check for bones, and cut off the fins.

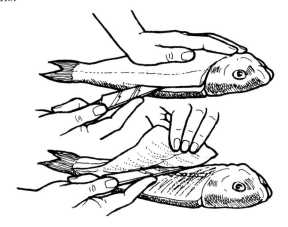

Boning

Herring, mackerel or trout: Remove the head and cut the belly right to the tail. Open the fish flat, and set aside the roe; then

place the fish, skin side up, on a board and press both sides of the backbone all the way down the fish. Turn over and pull the backbone clear, cut off end of bone and tail. Rinse and check for any remaining bones.

Skate: Fish other than the two main types may require a more specialized filleting technique. For instance, when preparing skate or any of the other rays, only the 'wings' are used for cooking. The skate wings are cut from either side of the backbone and cooked whole or cut into portions, depending on size; skate bones are large and pliable, so there is no need to fillet the wings. However, the dark skin is a problem and the sharp hooks embedded in the skin should be carefully cut out after skinning. Skate carry a good deal of natural slime and this should be scrubbed off first; then nick out the flesh along the thick side, just under the skin, to provide a purchase point. Use a strong pair of pliers to grip the skin and pull it off in one piece.

Dog fish or tope: These members of the shark family present the same sort of problem. The fish has a soft-boned (cartilaginous) structure so there is no need to fillet it. The skin, however, is very tough and needs to be removed before cooking. Gut the fish as for round fish and remove the fins and tail. To skin, follow the method described for eel (below).

Monkfish: Of the remaining soft-boned fish, the monkfish is the most common. At first sight the fish seems unattractive but the flesh is white, close-textured, and has much flavour. The large head should be removed where the definite shape of the tail commences. The meaty tail portion is easy to skin and cut into portions before cooking.

Eels: Both fresh-water and conger eels pose a slightly different problem in preparation. The larger sea-water species are difficult to skin, and are best cooked gutted and cut into steaks or fillets. The skin can then be removed after cooking.

Fresh-water eels, unlike other fish, live for a long time out of water. They are sold live, killed at the point of sale, and then skinned if necessary. If large, hang the eel up by a string round the 'neck', and make a cut through the skin all round the eel, just behind the head. Loosen the skin with a knife and pull the skin downwards over the tail. If small, just secure the head and proceed in the same way. Clean the eel after skinning and cut into sections across the body before cooking. The very small young eels-called elvers-can, however, be cooked whole.

Cooking fish

Fish is as delicate as egg white and must not be cooked for long, or at high temperatures. There are only a few tough fish which can be tenderized in a casserole. Once the fish has turned opaque, ie from raw translucent to a solid white, it is ready and should be served as quickly as possible. Further cooking only leads to shrinking and toughening. In general, oily fish lend themselves better than white sea fish to smoking or sousing. Lean white sea fish, with their more subtle taste and texture, are more often poached or used in delicately sauced dishes. River fish are sometimes thought to taste muddy, and are therefore often marinated or cooked with stronger flavourings. Fish steaks, thick fillets, and whole small fish, whether white or oily, from sea or river, are popular plainly grilled or fried, and served simply with plain or seasoned butter.

Frying
The most popular method of cooking fish is by deep or shallow frying.

Deep frying: For deep frying, the fish is normally first coated with batter, egg and breadcrumbs, or flour, and then fried in a properly designed, thick-bottomed pan with a suitable basket. The pan should contain enough clean vegetable oil or fat to cover the fish completely.

In deep frying fish the temperature should be between 180°–190°C/350°–375°F, depending on the fish to be fried. Use a frying basket for small, flour-dusted fish, to minimize spluttering.

Fish are particularly well suited to frying in batter. A good batter protects the natural flavour and texture from the hot oil, while the fish is cooked by the steam sealed inside the batter coating.

Do not use a basket for fish in batter because the uncooked batter will stick to the wires and spoil the look of the cooked fish. Use a large perforated spoon or broad slice to lift out the cooked fish. Always check that the fish is cooked through, especially any thicker pieces in a heavy batter. Test by piercing with a fine skewer to check that both the batter and fish are firm but tender right through. After frying, drain the fish on soft kitchen paper, and serve immediately.

Shallow frying: Shallow-fried fish are often coated first. The coating can be egg and breadcrumbs, flour, or, for scaled herrings, milk or beaten egg, then fine oatmeal. For the best results, use a heavy frying pan with a thick flat base. Oil or fat can be used, or equal quantities of oil and butter. Cook the fish slowly, letting the coating brown before turning the fish so it only needs to be turned once, which minimizes the risk of breaking it. Shallow frying takes 5–15 minutes, depending on the size of the fillet or whole fish being cooked. When shallow frying fillets, cook the flesh side first, and the skin side afterwards.

Fried fish should always be garnished and served with a piquant sauce to offset any oiliness. Garnish with sprigs of parsley, fresh or deep fried, and with lemon wedges. Tartare or Rémoulade sauce is good with most fish, Mustard sauce with grilled or fried herrings, and Gooseberry sauce with mackerel.

Grilling

Cooking in dry heat is a simple way of preparing whole fish, cutlets or fish steaks, and thick fillets. Oily fish respond particularly well to the heat from a kitchen grill or outside barbecue. In the kitchen, cover the grill pan with foil for easy cleaning. The grill must be preheated and the fish brushed or sprinkled with melted butter, margarine, or cooking oil, and seasoned inside and out. Make 3 diagonal slits in the skin of larger whole fish on each side, to prevent them curling.

Whole fish should be turned over once during grilling but fish steaks and fillets, unless very thick, will cook right through without being turned. Cook under moderate heat. Allow 7–8 minutes for thin fillets, 10–15 minutes for steaks and thicker fish. If you wish, baste fish with a savoury or herb butter while grilling.

Alternatively, marinate the fish before grilling. A simple marinade can be made up from oil and vinegar (or lemon juice) with grated onion or garlic seasoning, and a suitable herb such as dill, fennel, rosemary, thyme, sage or tarragon. Allow the fish to steep in the marinade for 1–2 hours before grilling.

After grilling, garnish the fish with chopped parsley and lemon wedges for flavouring, and serve with plain melted butter or a sauce such as Tartare or Rémoulade sauce.

A colourful dish can be made with small chunks of fish used as seafood kebabs. Really thick pieces of fish or shellfish, such as bacon-wrapped scallops, are threaded on long skewers with small tomatoes or onions, pieces of courgette, green pepper or other similar vegetables. Blanch the vegetables before making up the kebabs, to make sure they cook as quickly as the seafood.

Baking and sousing

Baking: Cooking smells are kept to a minimum when baking in the oven, and this helps to preserve flavour. There are many suitable ovenproof dishes with lids, including fish bricks in terracotta. For cooking in most ovenproof ware, the fish should be dotted with flakes of butter and then seasoned; add a generous squeeze of lemon juice and moisten with a very little fish stock or milk to prevent the fish sticking to the dish. Cover with the lid and bake in a moderate oven at 180°C/350°F/Gas Mark 4.

A good way to bake fish is to use the *en papillote* method of wrapping in foil. Even very large fish, like whole salmon, can be cooked in this way if the oven is big enough. Lay the fish on a sheet of foil which will enclose it completely. Add seasoning, butter, and a few drops of lemon juice, but no other liquid. Fold up the foil to make a parcel, and place on a baking tray in the preheated oven. Cook as above but check for readiness by piercing the thickest part of the fish through the foil with a clean skewer. A defrosted Pacific salmon cooked in this fashion, then skinned and decorated when cold, will be acceptable on any buffet.

Sousing: This is a simple method of oven-baking fish with vinegar to eat cold with salad. Oily fish, such as herrings, mackerel, and sardines are best. Herrings should be scaled and boned, then rolled up starting with the head end. Mackerel can be soused whole or filleted, but sardines can be cooked, and served whole. The usual garnishes for baked fish are parsley or watercress for colour and lemon wedges for a tang.

Poaching

Cooking fish in liquid gives a bonus in the form of well-flavoured fish stock. The liquid should never boil except when cooking live shellfish or trout in *au bleu* style, and then only gently, not a rolling boil. Poaching at just under boiling point, with the water only shivering, is enough for most fish; a higher heat will ruin their texture and flavour and create a smell. The fish should be poached in a suitable-sized pan with a well-fitting lid, either in the oven or over direct heat. Larger fish should be cooked in a fish kettle with a plate or rack inside on which to lift the fish out in one piece. Alternatively, line an oval, flameproof, pot-roaster or similar dish with a net of clean muslin, leaving the ends hanging over the side of the pot. Preheat the poaching liquid, making sure there is just enough to cover the fish, before adding small pieces or fillets; but put whole fish into cool liquid, and judge the cooking time from when the liquid starts to tremble. For fish to be eaten cold, just heat the liquid gently and maintain it for 5 minutes; then turn off the heat and allow the fish to cool in the liquid.

There is a two-way exchange of flavour in poaching. A well-flavoured and seasoned liquid will add to the flavour of the fish, and the fish will give up flavour to the liquid, making a particularly well-flavoured fish stock. It is important, especially for fresh-water fish, and fish which have been in the freezer for some time, not to use water or salted water alone, except for cooking shellfish. For simple dishes using white fish fillets or smoked haddock, poach in a half-and-half mixture of milk and water with a knob of butter, seasoning, and a bouquet garni. Use salt sparingly (no salt or herbs for smoked fish) because it may become concentrated in the cooking; it is better to taste and add later when the sauce is being prepared.

Reducing the fish stock (until it becomes thick and shiny) by heating it in an uncovered saucepan makes a strong fish fumet or glaze for use in sauces, and as a coating aspic. Take care not to reduce the liquid too drastically, because overcooking will spoil the fresh flavour and colour. Add salt to taste after reducing the stock. Fish stock or fumet can be frozen in any suitable container and preserved for later use.

Steaming

This is a good way to cook fish without fat, yet without making it too moist. It also avoids any risk of overcooking small thin fillets. It is useful for those on a light diet, or for precooking fish which will be finished in a sauce or served cold.

Take a plate which fits neatly on top of a saucepan, half fill the pan with water and heat until it boils; then reduce the heat so that the water only simmers. Place the plate on the saucepan and, if wished, warm a knob of butter on the plate until it melts, and add just a little water, wine, milk or lemon juice. Add any seasoning required; then put the prepared fish fillet on the plate and cover with another plate. Serve with a little of the liquid. The Chinese style of steaming fish in a properly perforated steamer has much to recommend it.

Stewing

This is a specialized casseroling method for fish which is the basis of fish soups, stews, and chowders. The fish is cooked in a seasoned liquid with vegetables and herbs to make a delicious basis for such dishes.

Home smoking

There are several makes of home smoking equipment available. Whole fish like trout and pieces of fillet can be hot or cold smoked, but for hot smoking they must be small. Most home smoking kits come complete with fuel, and the instructions cover the fish that are suitable.

Fish and the microwave

Fish and the microwave oven make perfect partners. For defrosting, cooking and reheating fish, the microwave is priceless and any fish cooked this way remains very moist and so full of flavour that it can simply be served with a wedge of lemon! By following these simple tips and guidelines, you will be both delighted and surprised at the range of dishes you can prepare.

Containers

As with all microwave cooking, you must *never* use metal containers. Boil-in-the-bags (when pierced before cooking), oven-to-table ware and containers especially made for microwaves are very suitable.

Frozen fish

The microwave is ideal for defrosting fish. It is so quick. Just use half the minimum cooking time for each side of the fish and remove the fish while it is still cold but soft. This will prevent the thinner parts of the fish from beginning to cook. It is best, if possible, to defrost the fish in the manufacturers' plastic wrapping, or just loosely cover the fish with a plate. If the fish fillets or steaks have been block frozen, it is best to allow them to defrost slightly out of the oven first so the fillets can be separated before being placed in a single layer in the oven. In order to ensure even defrosting, just turn the dish while in the oven or cover the thinner end of the fish with foil. After defrosting, rinse the cavity of the fish and put to one side to finish the standing time (see the following table).

Shellfish should be spread in a single layer on a plate. Halfway through the defrosting time, rearrange them.

Cooking

In order to ensure even cooking when cooking fish fillets in the microwave, arrange the fillets with the tails folded underneath themselves or overlapping each other pointing towards the centre. Whole fish should be cleaned and gutted in the normal way. Round fish, such as mackerel, should be placed on a plate, head to tail, and lightly scored in the thickest part of the flesh to allow the steam to escape. Turn the fish over half way through the cooking. If the thinner part of the fish is cooking too fast, just cover with a little foil. White fish can be brushed with melted butter or sprinkled with a little lemon juice to prevent any drying. However, avoid adding too much liquid because the fish will produce its own.

Cook all fish on maximum power unless the instructions for the microwave specify otherwise. As fish cooks very quickly, it is best to undertime rather than overtime. After cooking, allow the fish to stand for 3–4 minutes (see standing time in the following table). Remember that the fish will continue to cook after it is removed from the oven because of heat retention.

For fish recipes and the microwave, the possibilities are endless. White fish can be simply marinated in a little lemon juice and water, sprinkled with black pepper and some dill. On the other hand, tinned tomatoes, onion, garlic and fresh parsley will transform any fillet or fish steak. Serve fish on a bed of spinach, topped with grated cheese and a dash of cayenne for something simple and special. To make a wonderful stuffing for red or green peppers or aubergines, just chop some tuna or anchovies and mix with a little cooked rice, some herbs, chopped mushrooms and seasoning.

Defrosting and cooking fish in the microwave

Fish	Amount	Defrosting time	Standing time
Whole fish, gutted	2 × 200 g (2 × 8 oz)	8–9 min.	8 min.
Trout, herring	1 × 1.5 kg (1 × 3 lb)	15–16 min.	10 min.
Scallops	450 g (1 lb)	8–9 min.	5 min.
Shrimp, prawns	450 g (1 lb)	6–7 min.	5 min.
Mackerel	350 g (2 × 12 oz)	10–12 min.	8 min.
Fish steaks	2 × 175 g (2 × 6 oz)	4–5 min.	5 min.
Fish steak	175 g (6 oz)	2–3 min.	3 min.
Fish fillets	450 g (1 lb)	7–8 min.	5 min.
Cod, haddock			
Sole			
Crab	200 g (8 oz)	6–7 min.	5 min.

Freezing fish

Only the very freshest of fish and shellfish can be frozen, and this should be done very quickly. *Never* freeze fish bought from the fishmonger or from the supermarket because the delay in transporting the fish to the shops will affect both the flavour and preserving qualities of the fish. This is particularly true of shellfish, which must be freshly caught and frozen immediately.

All fish should be cleaned and gutted before freezing. Small fish, such as trout and herring, can be left whole but large fish should also have their heads and tails removed. Alternatively, fish cut into fillets or steaks can be wrapped in cling film and frozen.

White fish should first be washed in salt water and lemon juice to preserve the flavour and colour before drying, wrapping and freezing. Oily fish, however, should be washed in plain water as the combination of salt and oil would cause deterioration when in the freezer.

It is extremely important that fish is very well wrapped for freezing in order to protect it thoroughly from the air; to make sure that it does not break through the wrapping; and also to prevent the fishy smell transferring to other items in the freezer.

Prepare the fish and wrap in foil or cling film, making sure that there is a double layer of packaging between each piece of fish. This makes separation easy. Pack in plastic bags or firm containers, eliminating all air. Freeze as quickly as possible.

Plain frozen fillets and uncoated whole fish should be thoroughly thawed before cooking. Thaw in the wrapping or container, in the refrigerator. *Never* place the fish in water or hold it under running water to thaw it.

Store-bought breaded fish or fish in batter can be fried straight from the freezer. But always remember that the temperature of the oil or butter will be reduced by the frozen fish and this should be taken into consideration when timing the cooking.

Guidelines for freezing fish

Type of fish	Preparation for freezing	High quality storage life	Defrosting instructions
Crab, crayfish and lobster	Cook and cool. Remove flesh and pack in polythene bags or firm containers	1 month	Defrost in container in refrigerator and serve cold, or add to cooked dishes.
Mussels	Scrub and clean thoroughly. Put in a large pan over medium heat for 3 minutes to open. Cool, remove from shells, and pack in firm containers with juices	1 month	Defrost in container in refrigerator before adding to dishes
Oily fish (herring, mackerel, salmon)	Clean well, fillet, cut in steaks or leave whole. Separate pieces of fish with cling film. Wrap in plastic, excluding air carefully	2 months	Defrost large fish in refrigerator, but cook small fish from frozen
Oysters	Open and reserve liquid. Wash fish in brine (1 tablespoon salt to $\frac{1}{2}$ pint/ 300 ml water). Pack in firm containers in own liquid	1 month	Defrost in container in refrigerator and serve cold, or add to cooked dishes
Shrimp	Cook and cool in cooking liquid. Remove shells and pack in plastic bags or firm containers. Shrimp may be covered in melted, spiced butter	1 month	Defrost in container in refrigerator and serve cold, or add to cooked dishes
Smoked fish	Pack in plastic bags, wrapping individual fish in cling film	2 months	Defrost in refrigerator to eat cold, or cook haddock and kippers from frozen
White fish (eg cod, sole)	Clean, fillet or cut in steaks, or leave whole. Separate pieces of fish with cling film. Wrap in plastic, excluding air carefully	3 months	Defrost large fish in refrigerator, but cook small fish from frozen

SOUPS AND STARTERS

Fish soups and appetizers can be simple and economical, and nutritious and wholesome. In addition, they can provide a delicious start to a meal.

Salmon Chowder (opposite) is not only a very attractive and delicious soup for any dinner party, but it can be made in only twenty-five minutes! Flounder and Spinach Soup (page 24), which, served with croûtons and warm crusty bread, is a tasty and substantial meal in itself. Try the Fettucini with Tuna, Fennel and Orange (page 30), a quick and easy starter that is so unusual that it can double as a lovely luncheon served with a crisp salad.

Salmon Chowder

SALMON CHOWDER

12 small new potatoes, skins
 left on
2 shallots, finely chopped
1 bay leaf, broken
300 ml/½ pint milk
450 g/1 lb skinned salmon
 fillet
225 ml/8 fl oz fish stock
6 sprigs of parsley
50 ml/2 fl oz double cream
15 g/½ oz unsalted butter
salt and freshly ground white
 pepper
chopped parsley to garnish

Put the potatoes in a small saucepan that they will just fit in a single layer. Add the shallots, bay leaf and milk, cover and simmer for 12–15 minutes until the potatoes are just tender.

Meanwhile, cut the salmon into approx 3 cm/1¼ in pieces, then poach in the stock with the parsley for 2–3 minutes.

Remove the potatoes, bay leaf and as many of the pieces of shallot that can easily be scooped up from the milk with a perforated spoon and keep warm. Boil the milk until reduced to about 75 ml/3 fl oz, stirring occasionally to make sure that it does not catch on the bottom of the pan.

Meanwhile, lift out the salmon with a perforated spoon and keep warm with the potatoes. Boil the stock until reduced to 50 ml/2 fl oz.

Stir the milk and cream into the stock, remove the parsley and boil briefly. Reduce the heat and swirl in the butter. Season with salt and pepper and add the fish and potatoes. Turn to coat in the sauce, then serve garnished with chopped parsley.

SERVES 4–6.

CREAM OF HERRING AND OATMEAL SOUP

1 large onion, finely sliced
2 tablespoons oil
2 tablespoons oatmeal or
    rolled oats
2 herrings, cleaned and heads
    removed
600 ml/1 pint water or fish
    stock
2 bay leaves
salt and freshly ground pepper
150 ml/¼ pint single cream

Sauté the onion in the oil until transparent. Add the oats and stir well. Next add the herrings, water or fish stock, bay leaves and seasoning and bring to the boil. Simmer for 30 minutes. Remove the fish from the liquor and remove the tails, backbones and any other large bones. Place the flesh in a blender or food processor with the rest of the soup and blend until thick and smooth. Make sure that the bones have been blended. Add the cream and reheat. Do not allow to boil.

SERVES 4.

PORTUGUESE FISH SOUP

2 onions, finely chopped
1 clove garlic chopped,
    (optional)
2 tablespoons oil
450 g/1 lb canned tomatoes
juice of 1 lemon
2 tablespoons chopped parsley
1 teaspoon dried mixed herbs
50 g/2 oz vermicelli
600 ml/1 pint fish stock or
    water
salt and freshly ground pepper
8 fresh sardines, cleaned
4 slices French bread

Sauté the onions and garlic, if used, in oil until soft. Add the tomatoes, lemon juice, parsley, herbs, vermicelli, stock and seasoning. Bring to the boil and simmer for 15 minutes. Add the sardines and continue to simmer gently for 8–10 minutes until the fish are cooked through. Meanwhile toast the bread, searing it slightly. When the sardines are cooked, remove from the soup and keep hot to serve as the next course or leave to cool and serve with a salad the following day. Place a round of well-toasted bread in each soup bowl and spoon the soup over the top. Serve at once.

SERVES 4.

CONSOMMÉ CARMELITE

1.2 litres/2 pints strong fish
    stock
2 tablespoons uncooked rice
1 tablespoon chopped dulse
    seaweed
salt and freshly ground pepper

Place all ingredients together in a large saucepan and bring to the boil. Remove any scum and simmer for 15–20 minutes. Correct seasoning and serve with chunks of brown or black bread.

SERVES 4.

CACCIUCCO

4 tablespoons oil
3 cloves garlic, chopped
1 hot red pepper, finely
    chopped
1 onion, chopped
1 stick celery, chopped
1 can tomatoes
handful chopped parsley
salt and freshly ground black
    pepper
650 g/1½ lb mixed fish—
shrimp, prawns, clams, crab
    and squid, cut into bite-
    sized pieces
125 ml/5 fl oz dry white wine
900 g/2 lb mixed white fish—
    cod and halibut, cut into
    bite-sized pieces
4–8 slices stale Italian bread,
    toasted and rubbed with a
    cut clove of garlic

Heat the oil in a large saucepan, and cook the garlic and pepper until lightly browned, stirring occasionally. Add the onion, and celery and cook gently until soft, stirring occasionally. Add the tomatoes and parsley and season to taste and continue to cook, covered, for about 5 minutes. Add the mixed fish then pour over the wine. Cover, then cook for 30 minutes or until the fish is tender. Add the remaining fish and about 550 ml/1 pint of water, then cook for a further 15 minutes until all the fish is cooked.

Lay a slice of toasted garlic bread in each soup bowl and ladle the soup on top. Serve immediately. SERVES 4–8.

MEDITERRANEAN FISH SOUP

2 large onions, coarsely
    chopped
2 tablespoons oil
1 clove garlic, crushed
1 small mackerel, cleaned
225 g/8 oz coley
225 g/8 oz whiting or cod
450 g/1 lb fresh or canned
    tomatoes
2 tablespoons chopped parsley
½ teaspoon cayenne
1 bay leaf
grated rind of ½ lemon
salt and freshly ground pepper
1.2 litres/2 pints stock or water
150 ml/¼ pint white wine
powdered saffron

This is a version of the fish soup popular all along the coast of Provence, using easily available fish.

Sauté the onions in the oil with the garlic. Add all other ingredients except the saffron and bring to the boil. Simmer for 30 minutes. Take out the fish and remove the head, skin and bones and return the flesh to the soup. In a blender or food processor blend all the soup and add saffron to achieve the characteristic golden colour. Reheat and serve. SERVES 4.

Note This soup can provide the basis of a version of an English *bouillabaisse*, the French fish stew. When you have made the soup, simply poach mussels, prawns, red mullet and chunks of cod or hake in it for 10–15 minutes.

CRAB AND SHRIMP BISQUE

25 g/1 oz butter or margarine
1 small onion, finely chopped
1 small clove garlic, crushed
1 stick celery, diced
140 ml/¼ pint dry white wine
560 ml/1 pint fish stock
1 bouquet garni
1 bay leaf
*salt and freshly ground black
  pepper*
650 g/1½ lb shrimps, peeled
*650 g/1½ lbs brown and white
  crab meat*
140 ml/¼ pint single cream
1 tablespoon brandy
*140 ml/¼ pint natural yogurt
  to garnish*

Melt the butter in a large saucepan. Sauté the onion, garlic and celery until transparent. Add the wine, stock, bouquet garni, bay leaf and seasoning. Simmer for 5–10 minutes to allow the herbs to infuse. Stir in the shrimps, brown crab meat and half the white crab meat to simmer for 10 minutes. In a blender or food processor blend until smooth then return to the heat and add the cream, brandy and remaining crab meat. Before serving swirl with natural yogurt.

SERVES 4–6.

FLOUNDER AND SPINACH SOUP

*450 g/1 lb fresh spinach,
  washed and picked over*
*1 bunch watercress, washed
  and picked over*
*750 ml/1¼ pints water or fish
  stock*
1 clove garlic, crushed
salt and freshly ground pepper
*100 g/4 oz smoked mackerel
  fillet, skinned*
*450 g/1 lb flounders, cleaned
  and heads removed*
2 large slices bread
oil for frying

Remove any tough stalks from the spinach and watercress. Place in a pan with the water or fish stock and bring to the boil. Add the garlic to the pan with salt and pepper. Add the mackerel fillet to the soup with the flounders. Simmer for 20–25 minutes. Take the flounders out of the soup and remove all skin and bones. Place the flesh in a blender or food processor with the rest of the soup and blend until thick and smooth. Fry the bread in the oil, drain and leave to cool. Cut into small squares. Reheat the soup and serve with the fried bread croûtons.

SERVES 4.

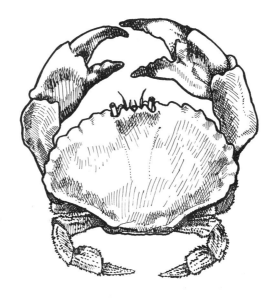

Kipper Soup

KIPPER SOUP

450 g/1 lb kipper fillets
2 × 397 g/14 oz can tomatoes
2 cloves garlic, crushed
2 tablespoons tomato purée
140 ml/¼ pint skimmed milk
freshly ground black pepper
natural yogurt to serve

Jug the kippers for 5 minutes, drain reserving the liquid. Skin and flake the fish into a blender or food processor. Add the tomatoes with juice, garlic and purée. Blend until smooth. Pour the mixture into a large saucepan and add ¾ pint/420 ml of the reserved liquid together with the skimmed milk. Bring to simmering point and simmer for 5 minutes. Serve hot with a swirl of natural yogurt.   SERVES 6.

NEW ORLEANS
BOUILLABAISSE

1 × 1.35 kg/3 lb red fish, sliced
   in 4.5 cm/2-inch strips
3 onions, finely chopped
2 red peppers, finely chopped
4 sticks celery, finely chopped
1 can tomatoes, chopped
450 ml/16 fl oz fish stock (see
   note below)
6 crabs, par-boiled, cleaned
   and halved
450 g/1 lb oysters
450 g/1 lb shrimp or prawns
450 g/1 lb crab meat
100 g/4 oz onion tops, finely
   chopped
25 g/1 oz fresh parsley, finely
   chopped
juice of 1 lemon
cooked rice to serve

In a large heavy saucepan, layer the fish meat with the chopped vegetables until all used. Add the tomatoes and fish stock and cook, covered, for about 1½ hours. Occasionally shake the pan to blend the ingredients but never stir. Add the crab halves, cover and cook for a further 30 minutes. Then add the remaining ingredients and cook for a further 30 minutes. Squeeze the lemon juice over the top and serve immediately over rice in soup bowls.   SERVES 6–8.

Note To make the fish stock, boil the fish head and bones with 1 carrot, 1 stick celery, bouquet garni and salt and pepper to taste for 1 hour. Strain and use.

CHILLED SCALLOP AND
WATERCRESS SOUP

4 scallops
2 bay leaves
150 ml/¼ pint milk
1 large onion, sliced
1 tablespoon oil
3 tablespoons sherry
2 bunches watercress, washed
   and picked over
1 large potato, chopped
400 ml/¾ pint stock
salt and freshly ground pepper
1–2 teaspoons cornflour
4 tablespoons double cream

Poach the scallops with bay leaves in the milk for 5 minutes and set on one side. Sauté the onion gently in the oil until transparent. Add sherry and bring to the boil. Add watercress, potato, stock, the milk from the scallops and seasoning. Bring to the boil again and simmer for 40 minutes. Put in a blender or food processor and blend until smooth. Return to the pan. Thicken with a little cornflour mixed with a little of the soup and bring to the boil. Remove from the heat and leave to cool. Place in the refrigerator to chill for 2 hours. Chop the scallops and add to the soup with the cream.
   SERVES 4.

CEBICHE

550 g/1¼ lb white fish—plaice,
  cod, haddock, sole,
  monkfish, scallops, or a
  combination
225 ml/8 fl oz fresh lime juice
75 ml/3 fl oz corn oil
50 ml/2 fl oz tomato ketchup
a dash of Worcestershire sauce
1 tablespoon fresh coriander,
  chopped
salt and freshly ground pepper
1 green chilli, chopped
3 tomatoes, skinned and
  chopped
1 medium onion, chopped

GARNISH
1 large ear of sweetcorn
leaves of cos lettuce, shredded
green olives, stoned
sprigs of fresh coriander

Skin, debone and chop the fish into small 2.5 cm/1 inch cubes and put into a glass bowl—*Note* The bowl *must* be glass. Pour the lime juice over the fish, and stir. It is essential that the fish be completely covered with the juice, as the juice 'cooks' the fish. Refrigerate for at least 8 hours. Stir occasionally. Meanwhile, cook the ear of corn in salted boiling water for 7 minutes. Drain and cool. Cut into eight pieces. Refrigerate until ready to use. Just before serving, drain the lime juice from the fish, reserving the juice. Put the fish to one side. Add the corn oil, tomato ketchup, Worcestershire sauce, chopped coriander, and salt and pepper to the lime juice. Mix well as for a vinaigrette. Add the chilli, tomatoes and onion to the drained fish. Dress with the sauce made from the marinade. Arrange the lettuce on individual serving plates, and spoon the fish mixture on top. Garnish with olives, pieces of sweetcorn and sprigs of fresh coriander.   SERVES 8.

Note *Cebiche* can be made solely with shellfish, or with a mixture of white fish and shellfish. The fish *must* be fresh.

CREAM OF SHRIMP SOUP

25 g/1 oz butter
25 g/1 oz flour
750 ml/1¼ pints strong fish
  stock
1 egg yolk
1 tablespoon double cream
salt and freshly ground pepper
75 g/3 oz peeled shrimps

Melt the butter in a pan and stir in the flour. Gradually add the fish stock, stirring all the time. Bring the mixture to the boil and simmer for 5 minutes. Remove from the heat and allow to cool a little. Mix egg yolk and cream and stir into the soup to thicken. Reheat but do not allow the mixture to boil. Season to taste and add shrimps. Serve at once.   SERVES 4.

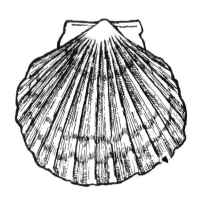

RAINBOW FISH SOUP

225 g/8 oz haddock fillet
4 dried mushrooms
550 ml/1 pint well-seasoned
    chicken stock
50 g/2 oz cooked shrimp or
    prawns
50 g/2 oz tomatoes, skinned
    and deseeded and chopped
    into 1-in pieces
50 g/2 oz bamboo shoots cut
    into 1-in wedges
50 g/2 oz mange tout, trimmed
    and cut diagonally into
    halves
3 slices fresh ginger
2 teaspoons rice wine
salt and freshly ground black
    pepper

THICKENING PASTE
2 tablespoons potato flour
3 tablespoons water

Remove the skin and cut the haddock into 3 cm/1 in pieces. Soak the dried mushrooms in warm water for 30 minutes, then discard the hard stalks and cut the caps in half. Mix the thickening paste in a small bowl. Bring the stock to the boil and add the fish, shrimp or prawns, tomatoes, mushrooms, bamboo shoots, mange tout and ginger. Bring back to the boil and add the rice wine. Season to taste with salt and pepper and simmer for 2 minutes. Mix in the thickening paste and serve at once.   SERVES 4.

WHITE FISH TERRINE WITH FENNEL

350 g/12 oz haddock
350 g/12 oz cod
150 ml/¼ pint milk or milk and
    water
1 small onion, sliced
1 blade mace
1 bay leaf
salt and freshly ground pepper
50 g/2 oz breadcrumbs
1 egg
¼ teaspoon fennel seeds
¼ teaspoon dried mixed herbs
fingers of brown toast to serve

Preheat the oven at 180°C/350°F/Gas Mark 4. Poach the fish in the milk or milk and water with the onion, mace, bay leaf and seasoning for about 8–10 minutes or until tender. Remove the haddock from the pan and take the flesh off the bone. Mash with a fork and mix with breadcrumbs and egg. Season well. Thoroughly grease a small terrine and pack half of the haddock mixture into the base of it. Take the cod from the cooking liquor and remove any skin or bones. Flake the flesh into small chunks and arrange on top of the haddock, pressing down well into the mixture. Sprinkle with fennel seeds, herbs and seasoning. Place the remaining haddock mixture on top and press down again.

Smooth over the top with a fork and cover. Bake in a tin of water for 1 hour. Allow to cool and turn out of the terrine. Serve in slices with fingers of thin brown toast.   SERVES 4–6.

Rainbow Fish Soup

LETTUCE MOUSSES WITH LIGHT SMOKED TROUT SAUCE

2 heads of round lettuce,
    quartered
225 ml/8 fl oz double cream
3 eggs
celery salt and freshly ground
    white pepper
lemon juice

SAUCE
50 g/2 oz smoked trout fillet
4 tablespoons cottage cheese
4 tablespoons thick natural
    yogurt
½ teaspoon lemon juice
½ teaspoon horseradish cream

Preheat the oven at 180°C/350°F/Gas Mark 4. Cook the lettuces in boiling water for 1½–2 minutes, refresh under cold running water, then press down firmly on them to remove excess moisture and chop.

Lightly whisk the cream and eggs together. Add the lettuce, celery, salt, pepper and lemon juice to taste.

Divide between 4 buttered individual ovenproof dishes. Place the dishes in a baking tin and surround them with boiling water about half way up the sides. Cover the tops of the dishes with greaseproof paper and cook for about 15–20 minutes until just set in the centre. Meanwhile, in a blender or food processor purée the ingredients for the sauce. Remove the dishes from the heat and leave to stand for a minute or two before unmoulding onto warmed plates. Spoon the sauce beside the moulds and garnish with sprigs of chervil or fennel.

SERVES 4.

FETTUCINE WITH TUNA, FENNEL AND ORANGE

25 g/1 oz unsalted butter,
    diced
1 tablespoon olive oil
1 small bulb of fennel, thinly
    sliced
350 g/12 oz fresh fettucine
    (see note)
salt and freshly ground black
    pepper
100 g/4 oz smoked tuna, sliced
75 ml/3 fl oz cream
1 orange, peeled, divided into
    segments, pith and skin
    removed
finely-chopped parsley to
    garnish

Heat the butter and oil, add the fennel and cook, stirring occasionally, for 2–3 minutes. Meanwhile, cook the fettucine in boiling salted water for 1 minute.

Cut the tuna into strips.

Drain the fettucine very well and return to the rinsed pan. Place over a low heat, then toss in the fennel and cream, then the tuna, orange, salt and pepper. Heat through gently for a minute or two. Serve sprinkled with plenty of chopped parsley.

SERVES 4.

Note Dried fettucine can be used if fresh is not available. Cook it before cooking the fennel for the length of time given on the packet.

LIGHT ROLLED OMELETTE
WITH FISH EGGS

4 eggs, separated
3 tablespoons finely-chopped
    chives
salt and freshly ground black
    pepper
175 ml/6 fl oz soured cream or
    thick Greek yogurt
2 heaped tablespoons salmon
    eggs or caviar
small lettuce leaves to garnish

Preheat the oven at 180°C/350°F/Gas Mark 4. Beat the egg whites until stiff. Break up the egg yolks, then gently fold into the whites with the chives, salt and pepper until just evenly mixed. Lightly spread the mixture into a 25 × 18 cm/10 × 7½ in Swiss roll tin, lined with well-greased greaseproof paper. Bake for about 6 minutes until set and pale golden.

Immediately spread the soured cream or yogurt over the omelette. Quickly sprinkle with the salmon eggs or caviar and roll up with the aid of the paper, as for a Swiss roll. Cut across into 12 slices and place, cut side up, on 4 small warmed plates. Garnish with the small lettuce leaves.   SERVES 4.

CRAB SUZANNA

1 onion, finely chopped
25 g/1 oz butter
175 g/6 oz canned white crab
    meat, drained
2 hard-boiled eggs, chopped
2 tablespoons chopped parsley
1 teaspoon Worcestershire
    sauce
1 teaspoon prepared mustard
¼ teaspoon cayenne
3 tablespoons double cream
salt and finely ground black
    pepper
50 g/2 oz brown breadcrumbs

Preheat the oven at 200°C/400°F/Gas Mark 6. Fry the onion in a little of the butter. Flake the crab meat and remove any membranes. Mix the hard-boiled eggs with the crab meat, onion, parsley, Worcestershire sauce, mustard and cayenne. Fold in the cream and season to taste. Spoon into individual ramekin dishes and top with breadcrumbs and knobs of butter. Bake for 20–30 minutes until crisp and brown on top.
          SERVES 4.

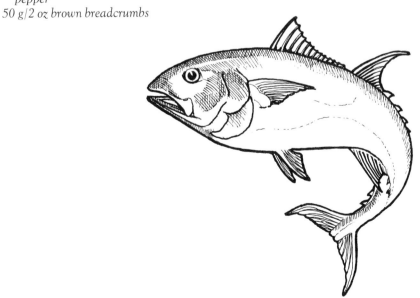

TUNA AND WALNUT PÂTÉ

75 g/3 oz butter, softened
200 g/7 oz canned tuna,
* drained and mashed*
25 g/1 oz walnut halves
2–3 shallots, finely chopped
1 teaspoon Worcestershire
* sauce*
salt and freshly ground pepper

Add the butter to the mashed tuna and mix well. Reserve 4 walnut halves for garnish and chop the remainder. Add the chopped walnuts, shallots and Worcestershire sauce to the tuna mixture. Season to taste. Press into individual ramekin dishes and chill. To serve, turn out and garnish with reserved walnuts. SERVES 4.

FRESH SARDINES STEAMED WITH SEAWEED

approx 20 g/¾ oz wakame
* (dried seaweed), soaked for*
* 5 minutes (see note)*
8 fresh sardines, cleaned and
* scaled*
freshly ground black pepper
4 tablespoons lemon juice

Squeeze the water from the soaked wakame, then place half in a layer in a steaming basket. Lay the sardines on top, season with black pepper then cover with the remaining wakame.
  Steam for 4–5 minutes until tender.
  Warm the lemon juice gently in a small saucepan.
  Arrange the wakame and sardines on 4 warmed plates and sprinkle them with lemon juice. SERVES 4.

Note Wakame or dried seaweed can be purchased at any oriental supermarket.

DRESSED CRAB

4 small 350 g/12 oz cooked
* crabs*
200 g/8 oz walnuts, finely
* chopped*
salt and freshly ground black
* pepper*

HERB DRESSING
200 g/8 oz low fat soft cheese
8 dessertspoons tarragon
* vinegar*
8 teaspoons chervil
8 teaspoons chives
8 teaspoons parsley
8 teaspoons basil
chicory and tomato salad to
* serve*

Remove the meat from the crab. Alternatively, use a prepared crab. Reserve the shell. Mix the chopped walnuts with the brown crab meat. Season with salt and pepper. Mix together the dressing ingredients and use 1 tablespoon of the herb dressing to moisten the white crab meat. Serve the remainder with the salad. Arrange brown and white meat alternately in the shell. Serve with chicory and tomato salad. SERVES 4.

MOULES MARINIÈRE

1.6 kg/2½ lbs live mussels
1 onion
1 carrot
1 stick of celery
1 bouquet garni
125 ml/5 fl oz water
125 ml/5 fl oz white wine
25 g/1 oz butter
1 tablespoon flour
freshly ground pepper
chopped parsley to garnish
crusty bread to serve

Scrub and beard the mussels, making sure that all are tightly closed, and put them into a large pan. Peel and slice the vegetables and tuck them among the mussels with the bouquet garni. Pour the water and wine over the mussels and place over moderate heat. Leave until the liquid boils up over them. Shake the pan 2 or 3 times and put to one side.

Blend the butter and flour together into a smooth beurre manié and put to one side. Strain the liquid from the pan of mussels, through muslin, into a smaller pan. Keep the mussels warm. Add the butter and flour mixture to the liquid in small pieces, whisking well. Heat until boiling, then season well with pepper. Put the mussels into a deep dish and pour the cooking liquid over them. Sprinkle with chopped parsley. Serve with pieces of crusty bread.   SERVES 4–6.

Moules Marinière

FISH CAKES

350 g/12 oz salmon fillet,
    skinned
sea salt and freshly ground
    white pepper
pinch of cayenne
1 teaspoon lemon juice

DRESSING
1 tablespoon lemon juice
3 tablespoons olive oil
1 teaspoon soy sauce
2 spring onions
salmon eggs or caviar,
    optional
coriander leaves and finely-
    shredded spring onions to
    garnish

With a very sharp flexible-bladed knife, cut the salmon into very small dice. Carefully transfer the dice to a cold bowl, sprinkle with sea salt, white pepper and lemon juice and toss lightly. Cover and chill for 30 minutes.

For the dressing, beat together the lemon juice, oil and soy sauce. Finely chop the spring onions and mix into the dressing. Drain the liquid from the salmon. Using hands, mould the salmon into cakes. Place on cold plates. If using salmon eggs or caviar, form a small indentation in the top of each cake and place a few eggs in the wells. Beat the dressing again, check the seasoning and spoon around the cakes. Garnish with coriander leaves and shreds of scallion.

SERVES 4.

SMOKED SALMON PIKELETS

2 tablespoons self-raising flour
1 teaspoon baking powder
pinch of mustard powder
freshly ground black pepper
1 egg, beaten
6 tablespoons milk
1 tablespoon melted unsalted
    butter
2 tablespoons finely-shredded
    smoked salmon
soured cream, lemon wedges
    and salmon eggs or caviar
    to serve
sprigs of parsley

Sift the flour, baking powder and mustard powder together and season with black pepper. Form a well in the centre, add the egg, milk and butter and mix with a fork to a smooth batter. Stir in the smoked salmon.

Lightly grease a non-stick frying pan with the butter. Heat over a high heat then add a tablespoon of the salmon mixture. Spread the mixture out lightly and cook for $1\frac{1}{2}$–2 minutes until bubbles rise to the surface and the underside is a light golden brown. Turn over for about 1 minute until the underside is browned.

Transfer to a warm plate and keep warm in a folded tea towel while cooking the remaining mixture. Serve as warm as possible with soured cream, lemon wedges and salmon eggs or caviar and with sprigs of parsley.

SERVES 4.

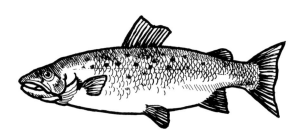

STEAMED SCALLOPS WITH CHIVE SAUCE

16 scallops
300 ml/½ pint fish stock
200 g/7 oz fromage blanc
1 tablespoon finely-chopped
    chives
¼ teaspoon Meaux mustard
salt and freshly ground white
    pepper
finely-grated lemon rind to
    garnish

Remove the scallops from their shells, separate the corals from the bodies and cut into halves horizontally. Place on a sheet of greaseproof paper in a single layer and steam for 2 minutes.

Meanwhile, boil the stock in a frying pan until reduced to 50 ml/2 fl oz. Stir in the fromage blanc, chives, mustard, salt and pepper and warm through, but do not allow to boil.

Spoon onto 4 warmed plates and arrange the scallops on top.

Sprinkle a little fine-grated lemon rind over the scallop bodies for garnish.

SERVES 4.

DEVILLED SCALLOPS

12 scallops
150 ml/¼ pint milk and water
150 ml/¼ pint double cream
2 teaspoons French mustard
1 teaspoon anchovy essence
½ teaspoon Worcestershire
    sauce
salt and freshly ground pepper
4 tablespoons breadcrumbs
butter to dot

Poach the scallops in the milk and water for about 4–5 minutes until tender. Drain and chop the scallops and place in a pan with the cream, mustard, anchovy essence, Worcestershire sauce and seasoning. Stir over a gentle heat until heated through. Do not allow the mixture to boil. Spoon the mixture into 4 scallop shells and sprinkle with the breadcrumbs. Dot with butter and place under a hot grill until the top is lightly browned.

SERVES 4.

SMOKED SALMON PÂTÉ IN ASPIC

225 g/8 oz smoked salmon,
    minced
75 g/3 oz butter, softened
4 tablespoons double cream
1 tablespoon lemon juice
freshly ground black pepper
150 ml/¼ pint aspic jelly
brown bread to serve

Mix the smoked salmon with softened butter. Add cream, lemon juice and black pepper and mix well together. Spoon into individual pots and place in the refrigerator to chill. After about 2–3 hours turn out the pâté and carefully coat with aspic. Return to the refrigerator to set fully. Serve with brown bread and butter.

SERVES 4.

SALADS AND COLD DISHES

When the long winter finally ends and the warmer, longer days of spring begin, what fun it can be to shake off the old routine of hot and wholesome winter meals and begin afresh with the crisp and colourful meals of summer. Fish provides the basis for a wide range of interesting and delicious salads and cold dishes (which can be enjoyed in winter too!).

Indoors and out, for luncheon parties, friendly get-togethers or family suppers, fish salads invite an enjoyable change to any meal. The Tuna and Chicken Salad (page 38) or the wholesome Kipper and Pasta Salad (page 38), are both filling meals in themselves. Tangy Cold Fish with Lemon Sauce (page 46) is simple to prepare and attractive and economical to serve. Lobster on the Half Shell filled with Russian Salad (page 47) provides something a little more exotic.

SHRIMP AND PASTA SALAD

100 g/4 oz pasta shapes
3 tablespoons oil
1 avocado pear, peeled and
    thinly sliced
450 g/1lb small peeled shrimp
1 tablespoon lemon juice
1 tablespoon fresh chopped
    parsley
$\frac{1}{4}$ teaspoon dried oregano, if
    liked

Cook the pasta in lightly-salted water until tender. Drain, cool and mix with the oil. Mix together the thinly-sliced avocado with the shrimp and mix in with the pasta. Add the lemon juice and fresh parsley and mix together carefully. Just before serving, sprinkle with oregano if using. Serve with fresh bread rolls. SERVES 2.

Shrimp and Pasta Salad

ORIENTAL FISH SALAD

100 g/4 oz rice
450 g/1 lb coley
milk to poach
3 cardamoms
1 bay leaf
salt and freshly ground pepper
225 g/8 oz smoked mackerel
    fillets
25 g/1 oz raisins
25 g/1 oz flaked almonds or
    pine kernels
2 teaspoons ground cumin
pinch cinnamon
1 teaspoon dried marjoram
1 tablespoon mayonnaise
1 tablespoon salad oil
1 teaspoon vinegar

GARNISH
2 hard-boiled eggs, thinly
    sliced
½ lemon, thinly sliced
chopped parsley

Cook rice in lightly salted water. Poach coley in a little milk with cardamoms, bay leaf, salt and pepper. When the fish is cooked, drain and leave to cool. Skin and bone the mackerel and coley and mash well with a fork. Mix with the cooked rice and all other ingredients and correct seasoning. Spoon into a bowl and garnish with eggs, lemon and parsley.

SERVES 4.

TUNA AND CHICKEN SALAD

1 × 1.5 kg/3 lb chicken
oil for roasting
salt and freshly ground pepper
200 g/7 oz canned tuna
150 ml/¼ pint milk
250 ml/8 fl oz mayonnaise
sprigs of parsley for garnish

Preheat the oven at 190°C/375°F/Gas Mark 5. Oil and season the chicken and roast for 1¼ hours until cooked through. Leave to cool and then skin and take the flesh from the bones. Cut into pieces and arrange on a large serving dish. Place contents of the can of tuna, including the juice, in a blender or food processor with the milk. Blend till smooth. Mix with mayonnaise and season to taste. The mixture should be thick and creamy. If it is too thick to pour, add a little more milk. Pour over the chicken and garnish with sprigs of parsley.

SERVES 4.

KIPPER AND PASTA SALAD

100 g/4 oz macaroni or pasta
    shells
3 tablespoons salad oil
350 g/12 oz frozen kipper
    fillets with butter or 3 fresh
    kippers
1 bunch watercress, washed,
    picked over, and coarsely
    chopped
1 small pickled cucumber,
    finely chopped
1 tablespoon vinegar
salt and freshly ground pepper

Cook pasta in lightly salted water until tender. Drain and mix with salad oil. Leave to cool. Cook kipper fillets as directed on the packet or poach the fresh kippers in a little water. Leave to cool and remove any skin and bones. Flake with a fork and mix with the cold pasta. Add the watercress and pickled cucumber to the pasta and kipper mixture with the vinegar. Season to taste.

SERVES 4.

PRAWN AND AVOCADO SALAD

Salt and freshly ground black
* pepper*
1 teaspoon vegetable oil
175 g/6 oz pasta shapes
225 g/8 oz peeled prawns
1 large avocado pear, sliced
1 tablespoon chives, chopped
juice and grated rind of 1
* lemon*
1 clove garlic, crushed
2 tablespoon vegetable oil

Half fill a large mixing bowl with boiling water, salt and black pepper and vegetable oil. Bring to the boil and when the water is boiling rapidly, immediately add the pasta and uncovered, cook for 5 minutes. Leave to stand for 8–10 minutes covered with cling film.

Drain, and when the pasta is cold add the prawns and avocado pear.

Make the dressing by mixing the chives, lemon juice and rind, crushed garlic and vegetable oil together in a screw top jar.

Pour the dressing over the salad, combining it well.

SERVES 4.

CARNIVAL CRAB SALAD

1 or 2 medium to large cooked
* crabs (enough to give*
* 350 g/12 oz meat)*
75 g/3 oz cooked pasta shells
75 g/3 oz cucumber, diced
3 tomatoes, skinned and diced
1 lettuce, washed and
* shredded*
salt and freshly ground black
* pepper*
lemon juice
150 ml/¼ pint mayonnaise
watercress and paprika to
* garnish*

Remove the meat from the crab, dice and mix together with the pasta shells, cucumber and tomatoes. Season to taste with salt, black pepper and lemon juice. Arrange the shredded lettuce in the base of glass dishes and divide the crab mixture between the dishes. Top each with mayonnaise.

Serve as a salad or starter garnished with watercress and a sprinkling of paprika.

SERVES 4–6.

PRAWN AND BEANSPROUT SALAD

4 tablespoons thick lemony mayonnaise (see note)
4 teaspoons Ricard or Pernod
1 spring onion, very finely chopped
225 g/8 oz peeled prawns
75 g/3 oz beansprouts
75 g/3 oz cucumber, diced
crisp lettuce leaves, shredded
½ teaspoon finely-chopped tarragon

This delicious salad can be made in just 10 minutes.

Blend the mayonnaise and Ricard or Pernod together, then add the spring onion.

Lightly toss together the prawns, beansprouts and cucumber.

Lightly fork the mayonnaise through the prawn mixture.

Divide the lettuce leaves between 4 cold plates and spoon the prawn mixture into the centre.

Sprinkle with the tarragon. SERVES 4.

Note Lemon-flavoured mayonnaise can be bought in most supermarkets.

WARM SALAD OF MUSSELS IN BLACK BEAN SAUCE

1 tablespoon oil, preferably sesame
1 teaspoon finely-chopped garlic
1½ tablespoons coarsely-chopped canned black beans
1 tablespoon finely-chopped spring onions
1 teaspoon soy sauce
1 tablespoon Marsala
75 ml/3 fl oz fish stock or water
¼ red pepper
curly endive or chicory
½ teaspoon cornflour
24 large shelled mussels, fresh or frozen

Heat a non-stick frying pan, add the oil, garlic, black beans and spring onions and stir together. Heat for a minute, then stir in the soy sauce, Marsala and stock or water. Bring to the boil and simmer for about 5 minutes.

Meanwhile, blanch and dice the red pepper and shred the endive or chicory.

Blend the cornflour with 1 tablespoon water, then stir into the sauce and cook, stirring, until the sauce thickens. Remove from the heat and carefully stir in the mussels to warm them through.

Place the curly endive or chicory to one side of 4 small plates. Spoon the mussels next to it and sprinkle with the diced red pepper. SERVES 4.

Warm Salad of Mussels in Black Bean Sauce

TUNA AND CHICKPEA SALAD

350 g/12 oz cooked or canned
    chickpeas
2 cloves garlic, crushed
3 tablespoons oil
1 tablespoon vinegar
¼ teaspoon chilli powder
salt and freshly ground pepper
1 can tuna, drained
12 black olives, halved
3 tablespoons chopped parsley
4 leaves fresh basil or ½
    teaspoon dried

Drain the chickpeas and reserve 1 tablespoon of the cooking or canning liquid. Add the reserved liquid to the garlic, oil, vinegar, chilli powder, salt and pepper and stir together well. Pour over the chickpeas and add the flaked tuna, olives, parsley and basil and toss well.   SERVES 4.

POTATO AND SHRIMP SALAD

900 g/2 lb fresh or frozen
    shrimp
675 g/1½ lb potatoes, diced
25 g/1 oz fresh parsley, finely
    chopped
25 g/1 oz fresh chives, finely
    chopped
5 anchovies with capers
200 ml/8 fl oz French salad
    dressing
cucumber slices for garnish

Cook and drain the shrimp, reserving a few for garnish. Leave aside until cool then chop into large pieces. Set aside. Cook the peeled and diced potatoes in boiling salted water until tender. Drain and allow to cool. Meanwhile in a blender or food processor combine the parsley, chives and anchovies until well blended. Add the salad dressing and mix until smooth. Add the chopped shrimp and potatoes. Mould the salad into a deep moulding dish and chill for about 1 hour. To serve, turn out on to a serving dish and garnish with the remaining shrimp and cucumber slices.   SERVES 6–8.

SALAD NIÇOISE

lettuce leaves
chicory or endive leaves,
    broken into pieces
4 sticks celery, trimmed and
    sliced
4 tomatoes, quartered
1 × 7.5 cm/3 in piece
    cucumber, sliced
2 beetroots, cooked, peeled
    and diced
8 small radishes, trimmed
12–16 black olives
3 hard-boiled eggs, quartered
4 anchovies
1 green pepper, deseeded and
    cut into rings
1 × 200 g/7 oz canned tuna,
    drained and flaked
80 ml/3 fl oz olive oil
2 tablespoons vinegar
freshly ground black pepper

Arrange the lettuce in 1 large or 4 small bowls and add the chicory, celery, and tomatoes, cucumber, beetroot, radishes and olives. Arrange the eggs on top of the salad with anchovies, green pepper rings and tuna. Just before serving, mix the oil and vinegar and pour over the salad. Sprinkle with black pepper.   SERVES 4.

SALAD MONTE CRISTO

2 dessert pears, peeled and
    diced
1 tablespoon mayonnaise
1 bunch watercress, washed,
    picked over and coarsely
    chopped
225 g/8 oz peeled prawns
25 g/1 oz flaked almonds
½ teaspoon dried tarragon
salt and freshly ground pepper
8 lettuce leaves

Mix the pears with the mayonnaise and add the watercress
with the prawns, flaked almonds, tarragon and seasoning.
Mix well and place in mounds on a bed of lettuce leaves.
Sprinkle with a little more tarragon on top before serving.

SERVES 4.

Note These quantities are sufficient for a small salad or
starter. Use 3 pears and 350 g/12 oz prawns for a more
substantial meal.

HALIBUT, ORANGE AND
WATERCRESS SALAD

4–6 halibut steaks
1 crisp lettuce
150 ml/6 fl oz mayonnaise
orange twists and watercress to
    garnish

COURT BOUILLON
1.1 litre/1¾ pints water
450 ml/16 fl oz dry white wine
1 tablespoon white wine
    vinegar
2 carrots, sliced
2 onions, sliced
2 sticks celery, chopped
2 parsley sprigs, finely
    chopped
1 bouquet garni
a few peppercorns
salt and freshly ground pepper

First prepare the court bouillon. Put the water, wine and wine
vinegar into a saucepan and add the carrot, onion, celery and
parsley. Add the bouquet garni, peppercorns and season to
taste, bring to the boil and simmer for 30 minutes. Leave to
cool and then strain.

Poach the fish steaks in the court bouillon for 7–10
minutes. Lift out, drain well and leave to cool. Remove the
skin from the fish. Shred the lettuce and arrange on a large
serving dish. Arrange the fish on the lettuce and coat with the
mayonnaise. Garnish with the orange twists and watercress.

SERVES 4.

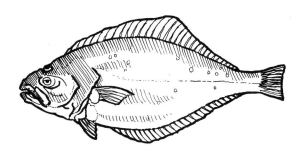

SALMON AND EGG LOAF

400 g/14 oz canned salmon,
  drained and mashed
100 g/4 oz butter, softened
1 small onion, grated
4 sticks celery, trimmed and
  grated
salt and freshly ground pepper
3 hard-boiled eggs, sliced
2 tablespoons mayonnaise
2 tablespoons chopped parsley
sprigs of watercress to garnish

Combine the salmon and the butter and cream the mixture. Add the onion and celery and season to taste. Grease a 450 g/1 lb loaf tin and spoon a third of the mixture into it. Smooth the top. Lay half the sliced eggs on top. Add 1 tablespoon each of mayonnaise and parsley. Next add another layer of salmon and repeat the layer of egg, mayonnaise and parsley. Finish off with the salmon. Place in the refrigerator and chill well. Turn out to serve and garnish with watercress.

SERVES 4.

AVOCADO PEAR WITH SMOKED OYSTERS

8 smoked oysters
1 just hard-boiled egg yolk
few drops Tabasco sauce
1 tablespoon lemon juice
3 tablespoons olive oil
salt and freshly ground black
  pepper
2 ripe avocado pears
sprigs of flat-leaved parsley to
  garnish

Drain the oil from the oysters. Mash the egg yolk, then gradually work in the Tabasco sauce, lemon juice and oil to make a thick, smooth sauce. Season with salt and pepper, taking care not to add too much salt.

Cut the avocado pears in half lengthways and remove the stones. Spoon a little of the sauce into the cavities left by the stones. Place 2 oysters in each cavity and spoon the remaining sauce over them. Garnish with sprigs of flat-leaved parsley.

SERVES 4.

TROUT IN PORT WINE JELLY

300 ml/$\frac{1}{2}$ pint port
300 ml/$\frac{1}{2}$ pint water
1 small carrot, sliced
1 small onion, sliced
1 stick celery, trimmed and
  sliced
1 bay leaf
salt and freshly ground pepper
mixed spice
4 trout, cleaned
15 g/$\frac{1}{2}$ oz gelatine
red food colouring

Place port and water in a pan. Add the vegetables to the liquid with the bay leaf, seasoning and mixed spice. Bring to the boil and cook for 15–20 minutes. Next poach the trout in this liquor until tender. Lift out the fish and leave to cool. Dissolve the gelatine in a little water in a basin set over a pan of hot water. Strain the liquor from the fish and add the gelatine. When the fish are cold, remove the heads, tails and skins and arrange the fish in a shallow dish. Colour the gelatine and cooking liquor with a little red food colouring and pour over the fish. Place in the refrigerator to set.

SERVES 4.

Lobster Mousse

LOBSTER MOUSSE

1 cooked lobster (about 900 g/
  2 lb) or 8 oz/225 g cooked
  lobster meat
juice of 1 lemon
freshly ground black pepper
3 teaspoons gelatine
275 ml/10 fl oz whipping
  cream
2 tablespoons mayonnaise
2 egg whites
strips of lemon and lime rind
lobster tail shell for garnish

Prepare the lobster if necessary. Using a blender or food processor, blend the lobster meat until smooth. Mix the gelatine with 3 tablespoons of water and dissolve over a pan of boiling water. Stir the gelatine into the lobster meat. Whisk the cream until thick and fold into the lobster meat with the mayonnaise, lemon juice and black pepper. Whisk the egg whites until stiff, fold into the mousse. Pour the mixture into individual mousse moulds that have been dampened slightly, and place into the refrigerator until firm. To serve, unmould the mousses and garnish with the lemon and lime rind and the lobster tail.   SERVES 4.

Note To make Crab Mousse, use 8 oz/225 g mixed crab meat instead of the lobster.

COLD FISH WITH LEMON SAUCE

1 onion, finely chopped
oil for frying
300 ml/½ pint water
1 bay leaf
½ teaspoon ground ginger
4 cod or hake steaks
juice of 1 lemon
2 egg yolks, beaten

Fry the onion in cooking oil until brown. Add the water, bay leaf and ginger and bring to the boil. Poach the fish steaks in this liquid until tender. When the fish is cooked, remove from the liquor and place in a shallow dish. Add lemon juice and egg yolks to the cooking liquor. Heat gently, whisking all the time with a wire whisk, until the mixture thickens. Pour over the fish and leave to cool. Serve the next day.   SERVES 4.

SARDINE AND POTATO PYRAMID

3 large potatoes
1 small onion, finely chopped
2 tablespoons salad oil
1 tablespoon wine vinegar
2 hard-boiled eggs, chopped
salt and freshly ground pepper
lettuce leaves
250 g/9 oz canned sardines,
    drained
juice of 1 lemon
3 tablespoons chopped parsley

Boil the potatoes and leave to cool slightly. Peel and dice. Mix the onion with the potatoes, oil and wine vinegar and leave until cold. Add the hard-boiled eggs to the potato mixture and season to taste. Pile the mixture in a pyramid shape on a bed of lettuce. Arrange the sardines standing up against the pyramid. Sprinkle with lemon juice and parsley.   SERVES 4.

POTTED SHRIMPS

50 g/2 oz butter
salt, nutmeg, cayenne
600 ml/1 pint peeled shrimps
50 g/2 oz clarified butter (see
    note)
3–4 lettuce leaves
lemon wedges to garnish

Melt the butter in a pan and sprinkle with salt, nutmeg and cayenne. Toss the shrimps in this until they are coated but do not cook at all. Pour into small moulds or ramekins and leave to set. Pour the clarified butter over the top of each mould or ramekin to seal and keep in the refrigerator for up to 2 weeks. To serve, turn out on to a bed of lettuce and garnish with lemon wedges.   SERVES 4.

Note To clarify the butter, put in a small pan and melt over a low heat. Skim off the scum that rises as the butter heats and discard, when no more scum appears, pour off the butter carefully.

MEDITERRANEAN COCKTAIL

½ small melon in season,
  peeled, sliced and cubed
175 g/6 oz green grapes,
  halved and deseeded
100 g/4 oz peeled prawns
¼ teaspoon dried basil
2 tablespoons mayonnaise
salt and freshly ground pepper

Mix the melon and grapes with the prawns. Sprinkle with the basil and toss in the mayonnaise. Season to taste. Spoon into individual glass dishes and chill before serving.   SERVES 4.

LOBSTER ON THE HALF SHELL FILLED WITH RUSSIAN SALAD

4 lobsters (about 450 g/1 lb
  each) cooked and split in
  half
1 lettuce
1 small cooked cauliflower
3 boiled potatoes
2 tomatoes
3 gherkins
4 tablespoons peas
2 tablespoons finely-chopped
  carrot
50 g/2 oz peeled prawns
salt and freshly ground black
  pepper
3 tablespoons mayonnaise

First prepare the cooked lobster. Place the lobster halves on a bed of lettuce leaves, reserving some lettuce for the salad, on four individual serving dishes, cut side up. Crack the claws and arrange them around the half-shell.

To prepare the salad, break the cooked cauliflower into small florets. Peel and dice the potatoes. Peel, deseed and dice the tomatoes. Chop the gherkins and shred the reserved lettuce leaves. Put all the ingredients in a bowl, add the peas, carrot, prawns, seasoning to taste and the mayonnaise and mix well. Divide the salad evenly and arrange on top of the lobster halves.   SERVES 4.

SALMON MOUSSE

25 g/1 oz butter
25 g/1 oz flour
300 ml/½ pint milk
200 g/7 oz canned salmon,
  drained and liquid reserved
15 g/½ oz gelatine
2 tablespoons white wine
150 ml/¼ pint whipping
  cream, stiffly whipped
5 cm/2 in length cucumber,
  thinly sliced
sprigs watercress

Melt the butter in a pan and stir in the flour. Gradually add the milk and the liquid from the can of salmon, stirring all the time. When the mixture thickens, cook for a further 2–3 minutes and remove from the heat. Finely mash the salmon and add to the sauce. Mix the gelatine with the white wine in a bowl and stand in a pan of hot water until the gelatine dissolves. Add to the salmon mixture and fold in with the whipped cream. Spoon into a wet 18 cm/7 in ring mould and place in the refrigerator to set. Turn out to serve and decorate with thinly sliced cucumber and watercress.   SERVES 4.

SEAFOOD FLAN

1 lemon sole, filleted and
    skinned
150 g/5 oz shortcrust pastry
225 g/8 oz peeled prawns
6 cocktail gherkins, sliced
1 × 150 g/5 oz jar cooked
    mussels, drained
300 ml/½ pint aspic jelly

Preheat the oven at 200°C/400°F/Gas Mark 6. Steam the sole. When it is cooked leave to cool and then cut into squares. Roll out the shortcrust pastry and use to line a 20 cm/8 in flan tin. Bake blind until golden brown and leave to cool. Arrange the pieces of sole and the prawns in the base of the flan and dot with gherkin slices. Place the mussels around the edge of the flan. Make up the aspic and pour over the flan. Place in the refrigerator to set.   SERVES 4–6.

SMOKED FISH QUICHE

150 g/5 oz shortcrust pastry
225 g/8 oz smoked cod or
    haddock or kipper fillets
1 large onion, finely sliced
oil for frying
75 g/3 oz grated Cheddar
    cheese
3 eggs
150 ml/¼ pint milk
salt and freshly ground pepper

Preheat the oven at 190°C/375°F/Gas Mark 5. Roll out pastry and use to line a 20 cm/8 in flan tin. Place fish in a pan with a little water and poach for 8–10 minutes. Remove from the cooking liquor, flake and leave to cool. Fry the onion in cooking oil until transparent. Arrange flaked fish and fried onion in the base of the flan and cover with cheese. Beat the eggs and milk together, season and pour into the flan. Bake for about 45 minutes until the top is golden brown and the quiche is set in the middle. Leave to cool for 20 minutes and then remove the flan case and place on a wire rack until completely cold. Serve with a crisp salad.   SERVES 4–6.

KIPPER AND MUSTARD SLICE

225 g/8 oz frozen puff pastry
350 g/12 oz frozen kipper
    fillets with butter
2 hard-boiled eggs, chopped
15 g/1 oz butter
25 g/1 oz flour
80 ml/3 fl oz milk
1 teaspoon grated lemon rind
2 teaspoons prepared mustard
2 tablespoons chopped parsley
salt and freshly ground pepper
milk for brushing

Preheat the oven at 200°C/400°F/Gas Mark 6. Roll out half the pastry to make a rectangular shape about 25 × 15 cm/ 10 × 6 in. Place on a greased baking tray. Roll out the second half of the pastry to a slightly larger size and slice across the centre to within 2.5 cm/1 in of the edges in lines about 1 cm/½ in apart. Cook the kippers as directed on the packet. Remove from the bag, retaining the liquid. Mash the kippers and mix with the hard-boiled eggs. Melt the butter in a pan and mix in the flour. Add milk and liquid from the kippers, stirring all the time. When the mixture thickens, add the eggs and kippers with the lemon rind, mustard, parsley and seasoning. Pile this mixture on to the pastry base and spread to within about 1 cm/½ in of the sides. Cover with the slashed pastry lid, sealing the edges with a little water. Brush with milk and bake for 30–40 minutes until the pastry is risen and golden brown.   SERVES 4–6.

Tomato Soused Herring

TOMATO SOUSED HERRING

4 herring, filleted
125 ml/4 fl oz bottled or
   canned tomato juice
2 tablespoon malt vinegar
6 green peppercorns
3 bay leaves
1 medium onion, thinly sliced
2 tomatoes, deseeded and
   finely chopped
salt to taste
lettuce or raddichio leaves for
   garnish

Cut the herring fillets into 2.5 cm/1 in pieces. Put the remaining ingredients into a large shallow pan. Add salt to taste and bring to the boil. Add the pieces of herring, cover and simmer gently for 5 minutes. Allow to cool and then chill thoroughly in the refrigerator. Serve garnished with lettuce or raddichio leaves. SERVES 4.

LONDON FISH LOAF

450 g/1 lb whiting
325 g/8 oz smoked cod
milk to poach
40 g/1½ oz butter
50 g/2 oz flour
2 eggs, beaten
freshly ground black pepper
cucumber slices to garnish

Preheat the oven at 190°C/375°F/Gas Mark 5. Poach whiting and smoked cod in a little milk. When the fish are cooked, leave to cool and then remove the skin and bones. Keep the cooking liquor for the sauce. Mash the fish with a fork and keep on one side.

Melt the butter in a saucepan and mix in the flour. Make up the cooking liquor with more cold milk to 300 ml/½ pint and gradually add to the flour and butter mixture, stirring all the time. When the mixture thickens, continue to cook for a few minutes then remove from heat and add the eggs. Next add the fish and black pepper. Grease a terrine or loaf tin and spoon the fish mixture into it. Place the terrine or tin in a tray of water and bake for 1 hour. Leave to cool. Chill in the refrigerator and then turn out on to a plate. Serve garnished with cucumber slices. SERVES 4.

MUSSEL AND ARTICHOKE VINAIGRETTE

225 g/8 oz courgettes, thickly
  sliced
½ cauliflower, divided into
  florets
1 × 400 g/14 oz can artichoke
  bases, drained
2 × 150 g/5 oz jars cooked
  mussels, drained
2 rashers lean bacon
30 ml/3 fl oz vinaigrette
  dressing

Steam the courgettes and cauliflower in a very little salted water for 6–8 minutes. Drain and leave to cool. Arrange on a plate with the artichokes and mussels. Fry or grill the bacon until crisp and dice. Sprinkle over the dish and spoon on the vinaigrette dressing. SERVES 4.

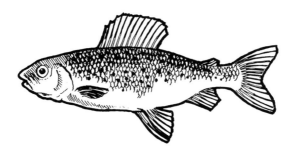

SMOKED HADDOCK MOUSSE

225 g/8 oz smoked haddock,
  skinned and cubed
140 ml/¼ pint water
1 teaspoon lemon juice
1 teaspoon gelatine
225 g/½ lb low fat soft cheese
freshly ground black pepper
1 egg white, stiffly beaten
peeled prawns, fresh dill and
  slices of lime to garnish

Poach the fish in the water and lemon juice for approximately 5 minutes. Drain the fish and sprinkle the gelatine into the hot cooking liquid. Stir until dissolved. Flake the fish until smooth using a blender or food processor. Blend in the soft cheese and the cooking liquid. Season to taste. Carefully fold in the beaten egg white. Spoon the mixture into 6 individual ramekin dishes and leave to set. To serve, garnish with peeled prawns, sprigs of fresh dill and slices of lime. SERVES 6.

TOMATO GALANTINE OF COD

15 g/½ oz gelatine
600 ml/1 pint water
225 g/8 oz tomatoes, skinned
  and sliced
1 onion, sliced
salt and freshly ground pepper
600 g/1¼ lb cooked cod, flaked
1 tablespoon chopped parsley
7.5 cm/3 inch piece cucumber,
  diced

GARNISH
2.5 cm/1 inch piece cucumber,
  thinly sliced
1 hard-boiled egg, sliced
lettuce leaves

Soak gelatine in 2 tablespoons of the water and place the rest in a pan with tomatoes and onion. Bring to the boil and simmer until the onion is tender. Blend in a blender or food processor and mix with gelatine and season to taste. When the tomato jelly is just beginning to set, mix in the fish, parsley and cucumber. Pour into a wet mould and leave in the refrigerator to set. To serve, turn out and garnish with cucumber and hard-boiled egg and surround with lettuce. SERVES 4.

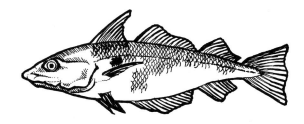

MAIN COURSES

The main course of any meal is the highlight of
the occasion. Whether it is for an elegant dinner
party, a special occasion with something to
celebrate, a family get-together or a quiet meal
for two, it is the all-important course.
Seafood Lasagne (page 55) can be made in
advance and served with a crisp salad and hot
French bread to soak up the juices. It will
delight guests and family alike. Fettucine with a
Duo of Salmon (page 57), is elegant and
beautiful to look at, yet it can be made in just
twenty minutes! The Plaice and Prawn Roulade
(page 58) is easy to prepare yet looks
magnificent.

Trout with Sage

TROUT WITH SAGE

4 trout, cleaned and rinsed
seasoned flour
75 g/3 oz butter
a few leaves sage
salt and freshly ground black
  pepper
lemon wedges to garnish

This is a very simple recipe enjoyed in the Tuscan hills and best made with freshly caught fish and sage picked on the way home from the trout stream! Let your imagination supply these ingredients should they be missing from your meal.

Roll the trout in seasoned flour. Melt the butter in a large heavy-based pan, and, when it begins to bubble, add the trout and sage. Cook gently for about 3 minutes on each side, according to size. Remove from the pan, season with salt and pepper, and serve immediately, garnished with lemon wedges.

SERVES 4.

COQUILLES ST JACQUES MORNAY

1 small onion
450 g/1 lb scallops
salt and freshly ground pepper
1 bay leaf
50 ml/2 fl oz dry white wine
75 ml/3 fl oz water
juice of ½ lemon
25 g/1 oz butter
25 g/1 oz flour
125 ml/5 fl oz milk
75 ml/3 fl oz cream
butter for greasing
200 g/6 oz mashed potato
3 tablespoons dried white
    breadcrumbs
4 tablespoons grated
    Parmesan cheese

Preheat the oven at 200°C/400°F/Gas Mark 6. Skin and slice the onion. Wash the scallops and place in a saucepan with the sliced onion, seasoning, and bay leaf. Pour the wine, water, and lemon juice over them. Poach gently for 5 minutes. Strain off the liquid and put to one side with the scallops.

Melt the butter in a saucepan, then stir in the flour. Blend in the liquid strained from the scallops, and stir over gentle heat until the sauce starts to thicken. Add the milk and simmer for 2–3 minutes. Stir in the cream. Slice the scallops and divide between 4 lightly-greased scallop shells or suitable small ovenproof dishes. Coat with the sauce. Pipe the mashed potato around the edge of each shell. Sprinkle lightly with the breadcrumbs and Parmesan cheese. Bake for 10–15 minutes.

SERVES 4.

PRAWNS MADRAS

25 g/1 oz butter
1 tablespoon oil
1 large onion, sliced
2 cloves garlic, crushed
1 tablespoon curry powder
½ teaspoon salt
½ teaspoon freshly ground
    black pepper
2 tablespoons lemon juice
150 ml/¼ pint fish or chicken
    stock
2 tablespoons tomato purée
50 g/2 oz sultanas
450 g/1 lb peeled prawns
long grain rice to serve
slices of lime to garnish

Heat the butter and oil in a large pan and fry the onion and garlic until soft. Add the curry powder and seasonings with the lemon juice to the pan and fry for 2 minutes. Stir in the stock and purée and simmer for 5 minutes. Add the sultanas and prawns and gently fry for a further 2 minutes. Serve with cooked long grain rice shaped into a crescent and garnish with slices of lime if available.

SERVES 2–4.

MARINATED SALMON STEAKS
WITH AVOCADO BUTTER

6 × 300 g/12 oz salmon steaks

MARINADE
1 clove of garlic
50 g/2 oz onion
125 ml/5 fl oz olive oil
3 tablespoons lemon juice
1 tablespoon Worcestershire
    sauce
salt and freshly ground pepper

AVOCADO BUTTER
2 ripe avocado pears
1 tablespoon lemon juice
100 g/4 oz unsalted butter
1 clove of garlic
1 tablespoon Worcestershire
    sauce
Tabasco sauce
salt and freshly ground pepper

Prepare the marinade first. Skin the garlic and onion and slice thinly. Mix together with the rest of the marinade ingredients. Put in the salmon steaks and turn them over to coat thoroughly. Marinate them in a refrigerator for at least 6 hours. Drain 15 minutes before cooking.

For the avocado butter, scoop out the flesh of the avocado pears from their skins. Discard the stones. Mash the flesh with the lemon juice to prevent discolouration; cream with the butter, blending thoroughly. Skin and crush the garlic and add it also. Add the Worcestershire sauce, a dash of Tabasco; and a little salt and pepper.

Grill the salmon steaks for 8–10 minutes, turning once. Serve with the avocado butter.   SERVES 6.

SEAFOOD LASAGNE

200 ml/7 fl oz single or double
    cream
1 egg, beaten
1 egg yolk
salt and freshly ground black
    pepper
2 teaspoons finely-chopped dill
100 g/4 oz fresh lasagne verde
    (see note)
6 clams
100 g/4 oz peeled prawns
18 mussels, shelled
75 g/3 oz monkfish fillet, cut
    into 2.5 cm/1 inch cubes
flesh of 3 tomatoes, chopped
15 g/½ oz freshly grated
    Parmesan cheese
15 g/½ oz unsalted butter

Preheat the oven at 180°C/350°F/Gas Mark 4. Bring the cream to simmering point, then stir into the egg and egg yolk. Season well with salt and pepper and add the dill.

Place a layer of overlapping pieces of lasagne in the bottom of a buttered shallow ovenproof dish. Cover with the clams, prawns, mussels and monkfish. Pour the cream over and cover with the tomatoes.

Cover with the remaining lasagne, sprinkle the Parmesan over and dot with the butter.

Cook for about 40 minutes until the centre is just set. Place under a hot grill to brown the top, if necessary.

Leave to stand for a few minutes before cutting into 4 square or rectangular portions and carefully transferring to warmed serving plates.   SERVES 4.

Note Dried lasagne can be used if fresh is not available. Check the packet to see if it has to be boiled first.

TROUT AMANDINE

4 trout, cleaned
seasoned flour to coat
100 g/4 oz butter
2 tablespoons oil
4 tablespoons blanched
  almonds
2 tablespoons lemon juice
2 tablespoons chopped parsley

Roll the trout in seasoned flour. Melt 50 g/2 oz of the butter with the oil in a frying pan and cook the trout until golden brown on both sides. Remove to a serving dish and keep warm. Drain the fat from the pan and melt the remaining butter. Add the almonds and cook gently, stirring, until golden brown. Add lemon juice and parsley and pour over the trout. Serve immediately.   SERVES 4.

FETTUCINE WITH A DUO OF SALMON

50 g/2 oz unsalted butter
225 g/8 oz skinned salmon
  fillet, cut into 5 cm/½ inch
  dice
3 tablespoons finely-chopped
  shallot
flesh of 2 tomatoes, chopped
100 ml/4 fl oz medium-bodied
  dry white wine
175 ml/6 fl oz fish stock
175 ml/6 fl oz double cream
5 tablespoons finely-chopped
  basil
350 g/12 oz fresh fettucine or
  300 g/10 oz dried fettucine
  (see note)
100 g/4 oz thinly-sliced
  smoked salmon, cut into
  strips
salt and freshly ground black
  pepper
basil leaves to garnish

Heat the butter in a frying pan over a moderate heat, add the fresh salmon and cook, stirring frequently, for 30 seconds.

Remove with a perforated spoon.

Add the shallot and tomato flesh to the pan and cook for 2 minutes, stirring occasionally.

Stir the wine and stock into the shallot and tomato mixture and boil over a high heat until syrupy. Stir in the cream and basil and boil until slightly thickened. Remove the pan from the heat. Cook the fresh pasta in boiling salted water for 1–2 minutes until just tender, but still firm to the bite. Drain the pasta well and keep warm. Quickly bring the sauce back to the boil. Add the diced salmon, then remove from the heat. Stir in the smoked salmon. Season to taste.

Mound the fettucine on four warmed plates, making a small well in the centre of each mound. Divide the salmon and sauce between the mounds. Finish with basil leaves, if liked.   SERVES 4.

Note If fresh fettucine is not available, dried can be used. Start cooking it while the shallots are cooking and cook for the length of time given on the packet.

Fettucine with a Duo of Salmon

PLAICE AND PRAWN ROULADE

15 g/½ oz butter
15 g/½ oz flour
150 ml/¼ pint milk
5 eggs, separated
salt and freshly ground pepper

FILLING
50 g/2 oz butter
50 g/2 oz flour
600 ml/1 pint milk
450 g/1 lb cooked plaice fillets
175 g/6 oz peeled prawns
½ teaspoon dried rosemary
salt and freshly ground pepper
sprigs of watercress to garnish

Preheat the oven at 200°C/400°F/Gas Mark 6. Line a 25 × 35 cm/10 × 14 in Swiss roll tin with greaseproof paper. Oil the paper well. Melt the butter in a pan and add the flour. Stir well and slowly add the milk, stirring all the time. Bring to the boil and cook for 1 minute. Remove from the heat and add the egg yolks and seasoning to the sauce. Whisk the egg whites until really stiff and fold into the sauce. Pour into the lined tin and quickly place in the oven. Bake for 15 minutes.

Meanwhile make the filling by melting the butter in a pan and making a sauce with the flour and milk as above. Remove any dark skin from the plaice and cut the fish into cubes. Add to the sauce with the prawns and rosemary and heat through. Season to taste. Remove the roulade from the oven and pour two thirds of the fish sauce over it. Roll up, removing the greaseproof paper as you go. Serve with remaining sauce. Garnish with watercress.

SERVES 4–6.

BAKED LEMON SOLE WITH PEMBROKE SAUCE

4 small-medium lemon sole,
    filleted
400 ml/¾ pint fish stock
1 bay leaf
salt and freshly ground pepper
1 onion, finely sliced
2 small leeks, trimmed and
    finely sliced
3 sticks celery, trimmed and
    finely sliced
12 button mushrooms
50 g/2 oz butter
25 g/1 oz flour

Preheat the oven at 190°C/375°F/Gas Mark 5. Roll up the fish fillets with the skin side inside, and place in an ovenproof dish. Pour on the fish stock and add the bay leaf and seasonings. Cover with foil and bake for 20–25 minutes until the fish is cooked. Very gently sauté the onion, leeks, celery and mushrooms in 25 g/1 oz of the butter. Continue cooking for about 5–8 minutes until soft. When the sole is cooked, drain off and reserve the liquid and keep the fish warm. Melt the remaining butter in a pan and stir in the flour. Add the liquid from the fish and bring to the boil, stirring all the time. When the sauce has thickened, add sautéed vegetables and adjust seasoning. Pour over the fish and serve at once.

SERVES 4.

SWEET AND SOUR PRAWNS

225 g/8 oz peeled prawns
1 tablespoon medium-dry
    sherry
salt and freshly ground pepper
2 onions
2 green peppers
2 tablespoons oil
125 ml/5 fl oz chicken stock
1 can pineapple pieces
1 tablespoon cornflour
2 tablespoons soy
    sauce
125 ml/5 fl oz white wine
    vinegar
75 g/3 oz sugar
unpeeled prawns to garnish

Marinate the prawns in the sherry for 30 minutes and season well. Skin the onions and deseed the green peppers. Slice them into rings. Heat the oil in a saucepan and fry the onions and peppers gently until tender. Add the stock then add the pineapple. Cover and cook for 3–5 minutes. Blend the cornflour, soy sauce, vinegar and sugar together, and add to the mixture. Stir until thickened. Add the marinated prawns, and cook for 1 minute.

Serve hot on boiled rice garnished with prawns.   SERVES 4.

SEAFOOD PAELLA

1 tablespoon sunflower oil
1 onion, finely chopped
$\frac{1}{2}$ green pepper, sliced
$\frac{1}{2}$ red pepper, sliced
225 g/8 oz long grain brown
    rice
large pinch turmeric or
    powdered saffron
560–840 ml/1–1$\frac{1}{2}$ pints fish
    stock
840 ml/1$\frac{1}{2}$ pints mixed
    shellfish—mussels, cockles,
    winkles and welks
225 g/8 oz cooked peeled
    prawns
salt and freshly ground pepper
12 whole prawns for garnish

Heat the oil in a large shallow pan. Fry the onion until transparent. Add the peppers, rice and turmeric and cook and stir for 2 minutes. Pour over sufficient stock to cover the rice. Cover the pan and simmer for 10 minutes, stirring occasionally. Add more stock if necessary. Meanwhile, wash and scrub the mussels and add to the rice. Cover and continue cooking for 5 minutes. Cook the winkles and whelks in boiling water and remove from the shell. Rinse cockles and peeled prawns. Stir in prawns, cockles, whelks and winkles into the rice. Cook for a further 5 minutes until the shellfish is hot, rice is cooked and mussels are open. Adjust the seasoning, remove mussels from shells, except approximately $\frac{1}{2}$ dozen which may be left as a garnish. Garnish with whole prawns and serve immediately straight from the pan.   SERVES 4.

SEAFOOD KEBABS

6 fresh scallops
8 whole prawns
1 large red pepper
1 large yellow pepper

MARINADE
140 ml/¼ pint sunflower oil
1 teaspoon fennel seeds
2 teaspoons fresh marjoram
2 teaspoons fresh thyme
2 bay leaves
juice of ½ lemon
salt and freshly ground black
    pepper
pitta bread or rice to serve

Slice the scallops in half. Using a cocktail cutter, cut 8 circles from each pepper. Thread fish and vegetables onto four skewers beginning and ending with a piece of pepper. Place in a shallow dish. Put all the ingredients for the marinade into a screw top jar, shake until well mixed. Pour this over the kebabs, cover and leave in a cool place for 1–2 hours, turning occasionally. Grill or barbecue kebabs for 5–10 minutes turning once. Serve in wholemeal pitta bread or with brown rice.

SERVES 4.

FISH FLORENTINE

750 g/1½ lb white fish fillets—
cod, haddock, plaice, huss or
    coley
salt and freshly ground pepper
juice of 1 lemon
1 bay leaf
150 ml/¼ pint water
1 kg/2 lb fresh spinach,
    washed and picked over
40 g/1½ oz butter
25 g/1 oz flour
200 ml/6 fl oz milk
25 g/1 oz grated cheese
1 teaspoon anchovy essence

Preheat the oven at 180°C/350°F/Gas Mark 4. Season the fish fillets and place in a shallow earthenware dish with the lemon juice, bay leaf and water. Cover with foil and bake for 20 minutes or until tender. Cook the spinach in a large pan in a little of the butter. Melt remaining butter in another pan and add the flour. Stir well and gradually add the milk and then the liquor from the fish. Bring to the boil, stirring all the time, and add the cheese. Adjust seasoning to taste. Place cooked spinach in the base of a casserole dish. Sprinkle with anchovy essence and then place the cooked fish on top. Pour the sauce over and glaze under the grill. Serve immediately.

SERVES 4.

CURRIED COD

350 g/12 oz cod fillets
50 g/2 oz butter
100 g/4 oz onion, sliced
1 tablespoon flour
1 tablespoon curry
    powder
450 ml/16 fl oz fish stock
1 tablespoon lemon juice
salt and freshly ground pepper
cayenne
rice to serve

Rinse the fish and pat dry. Cut into pieces. Melt the butter in a saucepan and fry the cod lightly. Remove the fish and keep hot. Skin and slice the onion. Add the sliced onion, flour, and curry powder to the butter and fry for 15 minutes, stirring all the time to prevent the onion becoming too brown. Pour in the stock and stir until boiling; reduce the heat and simmer gently for 20 minutes. Strain and return to the saucepan, add the lemon juice and seasoning to taste, bring nearly to boiling point, and then put in the fish.

Cover and heat gently until the fish has absorbed the flavour of the sauce. Stir occasionally to avoid sticking. Serve with boiled rice.

SERVES 5–6.

Seafood Kebabs

POACHED MACKEREL WITH LEMON AND GOOSEBERRY SAUCE

4 small mackerel, cleaned
1 onion, chopped
1 carrot, chopped
1 bay leaf
salt and freshly ground pepper

SAUCE
25 g/1 oz butter
25 g/1 oz flour
225 g/8 oz gooseberries,
   cooked and puréed
1 tablespoon chopped chives
juice of 1 lemon

Place the mackerel in a pan and cover with water. Add the onion, carrot and bay leaf. Season and bring to the boil. Turn down the heat and simmer for about 10 minutes until the fish are tender. Remove the fish and reserve the liquor.

Make the sauce by melting the butter in another pan. Add the flour and stir well. Next add 150 ml/$\frac{1}{4}$ pint of strained fish stock from the mackerel and the cooked and puréed gooseberries. Bring to the boil, stirring all the time. Add chives, lemon juice and seasoning and cook for 5 minutes. Serve with the mackerel. SERVES 4.

SOLE VÉRONIQUE

3–4 Dover sole, filleted and
skinned
150 ml/¼ pint water
150 ml/¼ pint dry white wine
4 peppercorns
½ onion, sliced
25 g/1 oz butter
25 g/1 oz flour
salt and freshly ground pepper
2 egg yolks
100 ml/4 fl oz single cream
175 g/6 oz green grapes,
peeled, halved and
deseeded
chopped parsley to garnish

Preheat the oven at 180°C/350°F/Gas Mark 4. Butter an ovenproof dish and fold the sole fillets over in it *en cravate*. Pour over the water and the wine. Add the peppercorns and onion, cover and cook in the oven for about 15 minutes. Melt the butter and stir in the flour. Cook for 2–3 minutes. Strain the liquor from the fish and gradually add to the flour mixture. Stir over a gentle heat until boiling. Season and remove from heat. Mix the egg yolks with the cream and add to the sauce. Thicken over the heat but do not allow to boil. Add the grapes, and pour over the sole. Sprinkle with chopped parsley, and serve immediately.   SERVES 4.

SALMON CUTLETS WITH CUCUMBER SAUCE

4 salmon cutlets
1 onion, chopped
1 carrot, chopped
1 bay leaf
1 teaspoon oil
salt and freshly ground pepper

SAUCE
¼ medium cucumber, cubed
80 ml/3 fl oz natural yogurt
1½ tablespoons cornflour
15 g/½ oz butter

Place the salmon cutlets in a pan and just cover with water. Add the onion and carrot, bay leaf, oil and seasonings. Bring slowly to the boil and boil for 1 minute. Turn off the heat and leave to stand for 5 minutes.

To make the sauce, put the cucumber, yogurt and cornflour in a blender or food processor and blend until very smooth. Melt the butter in a small saucepan. Pour in the cucumber mixture and bring to the boil, stirring all the time. Continue to cook for 2–3 minutes and season to taste. Drain the cutlets and serve with the sauce.   SERVES 4.

LOBSTER NEWBURG

3 cooked lobsters, split
lengthways
50 g/2 oz butter
3 tablespoons heated brandy
2 egg yolks, beaten
300 ml/½ pint double cream
salt and freshly ground pepper
paprika
cayenne

Remove the meat from the lobsters and cut into large chunks. Sauté in butter for a few minutes. Add the brandy and flame. Mix the egg yolks with the cream. Place in the top of a double saucepan and cook over water, stirring all the time, until the mixture coats the spoon. Add the lobster meat, pan juices and seasonings. Heat through, taking care not to curdle the sauce. Serve on a bed of rice or fried bread, or in vol-au-vents.

SERVES 4.

TROUT PROVENÇALE

1 onion, chopped
1 clove garlic, chopped
olive oil for frying
1 red pepper, deseeded and
    coarsely chopped
6–8 tomatoes, skinned and
    chopped
150 ml/¼ pint fish stock
¼ teaspoon dried thyme
1 teaspoon tomato purée
salt and freshly ground pepper
4 trout, cleaned
chopped parsley to garnish

Sauté the onion and garlic in olive oil until transparent. Add the coarsely chopped pepper, tomatoes, fish stock, thyme, tomato purée and seasoning. Bring to the boil and simmer for 15–20 minutes until all the vegetables are soft. In a blender or food processor, purée and return to the heat. The purée should be fairly thick. Poach trout and when they are cooked, drain and skin. Arrange on a serving dish and pour the vegetable purée over the top. Garnish with parsley and serve at once.   SERVES 4.

BAKED FISH STUFFED WITH HERBS

1 × 675–900 g/1½–2 lb trout,
    grey mullet or whiting

STUFFING
6 medium onions, sliced
3 tablespoons oil
2 cloves garlic, crushed
½ teaspoon turmeric
½ teaspoon salt
bunch fresh fenugreek,
    chopped or bunch of fresh
    parsley, chopped and a
    pinch of ground fenugreek
juice of 3 lemons
lettuce leaves, shredded
long grain rice to serve
lemon slices to garnish

Preheat the oven at 190°C/375°F/Gas Mark 4. Cut the fish open on the underside from head to tail, leaving the head on. Gently press out the backbone and remove any remaining bones. Place in an ovenproof dish.

For the stuffing, fry the onions in the oil until golden-brown. Add the garlic, turmeric and salt, and fry for a further 1–2 minutes. Mix in the fenugreek or parsley and ground fenugreek and lemon juice. Cook for 5 minutes. Push the stuffing inside the fish, reserving a little to cover the top layer of skin. Cover with foil, and bake in the fairly hot oven for 20 minutes, then uncover for 10 minutes until the flesh is cooked. Carefully remove the layer of stuffing covering the skin. Serve the fish on a bed of shredded lettuce and long grain rice, garnished with lemon slices.   SERVES 4–6.

FILLETS OF SOLE WITH CUMIN

3–4 Dover or lemon soles,
  filleted and skinned
300 ml/½ pint white wine
1 bay leaf
25 g/1 oz butter
25 g/1 oz flour
1 tablespoon tomato purée
1–2 teaspoons ground cumin
salt and freshly ground pepper
3 tablespoons double cream
watercress sprigs to garnish

Poach the sole very gently in the white wine with the bay leaf for 6–8 minutes until cooked. Place the fish on a serving dish and keep warm. Melt the butter in a saucepan and add the flour. Stir well and gradually add the liquor from the fish. Bring to the boil, stirring all the time, and add tomato purée, cumin and seasoning to taste. Simmer for 8 minutes. Add the cream, pour over the fish and garnish with watercress.

SERVES 4.

BAKED STUFFED FRESHWATER BREAM

1 large freshwater bream,
  cleaned

STUFFING
225 g/8 oz whiting, cleaned
25 g/1 oz bacon fat
2 rashers streaky bacon, finely
  diced
100 g/4 oz cooked rice
1 egg, beaten
¼ teaspoon dried mixed herbs
salt and freshly ground pepper

Preheat the oven at 180°C/350°F/Gas Mark 4. Soak the bream in salt water overnight in the refrigerator. Wash and dry the bream. Make the stuffing by poaching the whiting and removing the bones and skin. Flake the fish and mash with a fork. Melt the bacon fat in a pan and fry the bacon. Drain on kitchen paper and mix with the fish. Mix in the rice, egg and herbs. Season to taste. Stuff the belly of the bream with this mixture and sew up the cavity. Place in an ovenproof dish and pour the remaining bacon fat over the top. Bake for 45 minutes, basting every 10 minutes.

SERVES 4.

BAKED RED MULLET

4 large or 8 medium red
  mullet, cleaned and scaled
1 teaspoon dried fennel or
  fennel seed
salt and freshly ground pepper
juice of 2 lemons

Preheat the oven at 180°C/350°F/Gas Mark 4. Make sure all scales have been removed from the fish. Sprinkle the inside of fish with fennel and seasoning. Fold each in oiled greaseproof paper and bake for 35 minutes for large fish and 25 minutes for medium fish. Strip the paper off the fish and serve with the liquor that has oozed from the fish mixed with heated lemon juice.

SERVES 4.

Chinese Carp

CHINESE CARP

1 × 675 g/1½ lb carp, scaled
and gutted with head and
tail left on
1 teaspoon salt
cornflour for dusting
6 spring onions, cut into very
fine threads
3 tablespoons fresh ginger cut
into fine threads

STUFFING
3 dried mushrooms
100 g/4 oz lean pork, minced
4 fresh shelled shrimps, veins
removed and chopped
½ teaspoon salt
2 teaspoon sesame oil
1 teaspoon cornflour
2 teaspoons rice wine
pinch of black pepper

SEASONING SAUCE
2 tablespoons sesame oil
2 tablespoons soy sauce

First prepare the stuffing by soaking the mushrooms in hot water for 30 minutes and then discarding the hard stalks and chopping the caps finely. Blend all the ingredients for the stuffing together very thoroughly. Pat the fish dry and sprinkle the skin with salt before dusting it inside and out with the cornflour. Fill the stomach cavity with the prepared stuffing, folding the thin flaps of skin over to close. Lay the fish carefully on to a dish and put in a steamer over fast boiling water. Steam for 30–40 minutes until the eyes puff up and the fish is cooked.

Slide the fish carefully on to a heated serving dish and sprinkle over it the onion and ginger threads. Heat the sesame oil and soy sauce in a small saucepan and, when boiling, pour quickly over the ginger and onion and serve at once.   SERVES 6.

MONKFISH AND BROAD BEAN RAGOÛT

25 g/1 oz unsalted butter
2 tablespoons finely-chopped shallots
700 g/1½ lb boned monkfish tail, skinned and cut into approx 3 cm/1¼ inch cubes
350 g/12 oz shelled young broad beans, or thawed frozen broad beans
1 sprig of summer savory
175 ml/6 fl oz medium-bodied dry white wine
175 ml/6 fl oz crème fraîche
salt and freshly ground white pepper
4 teaspoons finely-chopped savory to garnish

Heat the butter, add the shallots and cook over a moderately low heat for about 3 minutes. Add the fish and cook over a moderate heat, stirring occasionally, for 2 minutes.

Meanwhile, blanch the broad beans (if using fresh beans) in boiling salted water for 1 minute. Drain well. Add the beans to the fish with the savory and wine, cover and cook gently for about 3 minutes until the beans and fish are just tender. Transfer the fish and beans to a warmed plate with a perforated spoon. Boil the cooking juices with the savory until reduced to a light syrupy consistency. Stir in the crème fraîche and boil to reduce to a smooth sauce. Adjust the seasoning, remove the savory and spoon the sauce over the fish and beans. Sprinkle over a little more chopped savory.

SERVES 4.

HAKE WITH ORANGE AND DILL SAUCE

4 × 125–225 g/6–8 oz hake steaks
280 ml/½ pint fish or chicken stock
1 tablespoon fresh dill
salt and freshly ground black pepper
1 tablespoon cornflour
70 ml/3 fl oz concentrated Florida orange juice
2 oranges, peeled and cut into segments
fresh dill to garnish

Poach the hake steaks in the fish or chicken stock with the dill and seasoning for 8–10 minutes. Drain and transfer to a warmed serving dish, reserving the poaching liquid. Mix the cornflour to a paste with the orange juice and add to the poaching liquid with the orange segments. Cook stirring, until thickened and hot. Spoon some of the sauce over the fish and garnish with fresh dill. Serve remaining sauce separately.

SERVES 4.

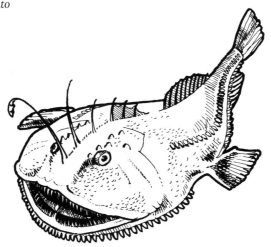

LOBSTER THERMIDOR

2 cooked lobsters, split
   lengthways
300 ml/½ pint dry white wine
300 ml/½ pint fish stock
1 onion, sliced
300 ml/½ pint milk
1 sprig thyme wrapped in leek
   leaves
salt and freshly ground pepper
cayenne
65 g/2½ oz butter
40 g/1½ oz flour
1 teaspoon prepared mustard
1 egg yolk
80 ml/3 fl oz single cream
50 g/2 oz grated Parmesan
   cheese
25 g/1 oz dried breadcrumbs
lettuce leaves to serve

Remove the meat from the lobsters and cut into large chunks. Rub any loose coral through a fine sieve and place on one side. Pour wine and stock into a pan and boil rapidly until it is reduced to 150 ml/¼ pint. Place the onion in another pan with milk, thyme, salt and pepper. Bring to the boil and remove from the heat. Leave to stand for about 20 minutes. Then melt 40 g/1½ oz butter in a pan and stir in the flour. Gradually add the reduced wine and fish stock and the strained milk, stirring all the time. Bring to the boil and cook for 2–3 minutes. Meanwhile melt the remaining butter and toss the lobster in it but do not allow to cook.

Remove lobster and sauce from the heat and mix together. Add cayenne, mustard, sieved coral, egg yolk and cream and correct seasoning if necessary. Spoon the mixture back into the lobster shells. Mix Parmesan and dried breadcrumbs and sprinkle over the lobster mixture. Place under a high grill to brown. Serve on a bed of lettuce.   SERVES 4.

SWEET AND SOUR HERRING

4 herrings, filleted
150 ml/¼ pint white vinegar
4 tablespoons water
75 g/3 oz caster sugar
1 teaspoon soy sauce
2 medium carrots, thinly sliced
1 medium onion, thinly sliced
1 slice fresh or canned
   pineapple, chopped
1 red pepper, deseeded and cut
   into thin strips
6 peppercorns
2 bay leaves

Preheat oven at 180°C/350°F/Gas Mark 4. Roll up the herrings from head to tail and place close together in a deep ovenproof dish. Place the remaining ingredients in a saucepan and heat slowly until the sugar is dissolved. Pour the mixture over the herrings, cover and bake for 30 minutes. Cool in cooking liquid and serve chilled.   SERVES 4.

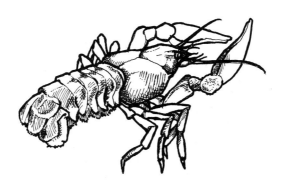

SNACKS AND SUPPERS

Fish dishes are ideal for snacks and suppers: the simple but tasty snack to satisfy that hunger in between meals; the cozy evening supper for family and friends with no formalities, just good food and good conversation; the quick but tasty and filling meal prepared after a hard day's work; the hearty and wholesome casserole to prepare in advance and eat when the time is right.

The Prawn and Cottage Cheese Soufflé (page 69) will prove just how easy a light and airy soufflé can be. Try the Stuffed Baked Potatoes (page 72), the children will love them and you will probably think of some extra fillings. The Wholemeal Fish Crêpes (page 73) are simply delicious and very quick, especially when the pancakes are made in advance and kept in the freezer.

Prawn and Cottage Cheese Soufflé

PRAWN AND COTTAGE
CHEESE SOUFFLÉ

25 g/1 oz butter or margarine
25 g/1 oz plain flour
280 ml/½ pint milk
salt and freshly ground black pepper
100 g/4 oz cottage cheese with chives
450 g/1 lb cooked peeled prawns, rinsed
2 tablespoons fresh chopped parsley
4 eggs, separated
1.7 litre/3 pint soufflé dish

Preheat the oven to 180°C/350°F/Gas Mark 4. Melt the butter in a saucepan, stir in the flour and cook for 1 minute. Remove from the heat, gradually add the milk. Stir over a gentle heat until the sauce thickens and season. Beat in the egg yolks. Stir in the cottage cheese, prawns (reserving some for garnish) and parsley. Whisk the egg whites until stiff, fold into the mixture. Pour into the buttered soufflé dish and sprinkle with the reserved prawns. Bake for 30–35 minutes until well risen and golden brown. Serve immediately. SERVES 4.

SHRIMP AND PEPPER OMELETTE

225 g/8 oz peeled shrimps or
   prawns
75 g/3 oz canned or bottled
   pimentos, drained and
   chopped
15 g/½ oz butter
7 eggs
1 tablespoon water
salt and freshly ground pepper

Place shrimps or prawns in a pan with pimentos and butter and warm through. Do not allow to overheat or the shrimps will toughen. Beat eggs with the water and season. Pour the eggs into a hot buttered frying pan and cook quickly, stirring a little. When the omelette is almost cooked, sprinkle the shrimps and pimentos over the top and fold up. Serve at once.   SERVES 3–4.

KEDGEREE

2 hard-boiled eggs, chopped
450 g/1 lb cooked smoked
   haddock or cod, skinned,
   boned and flaked
225 g/8 oz cooked rice
2 tablespoons lemon juice
salt and freshly ground black
   pepper
nutmeg
150 ml/¼ pint single cream
50 g/2 oz butter
2 tablespoons chopped parsley

Preheat the oven at 180°C/350°F/Gas Mark 4. Mix the hard-boiled eggs with the fish and rice. Add the lemon juice and seasonings, and stir in the single cream. Butter an ovenproof dish and turn the mixture into it. Dot with the butter and bake for about 30 minutes. Stir in the parsley and serve.
                                  SERVES 4.

SMOKED HADDOCK AND GREEN PEA QUICHE

150 g/5 oz shortcrust pastry
100 g/4 oz smoked haddock
milk to poach
175 g/6 oz frozen peas
75 g/3 oz grated Cheddar
   cheese
3 eggs, beaten
150 ml/¼ pint single cream
salt and freshly ground pepper

Preheat the oven at 190°C/375°F/Gas Mark 5. Roll out the pastry and use to line an 18 cm/7 in flan tin. Place the smoked haddock in a pan with a little milk and poach for 10 minutes until cooked. Remove fish from the milk, flake and leave to cool; reserve the liquor. Thaw peas for 2 minutes in boiling water and drain. Place haddock and peas in the base of the flan. Cover with cheese. Beat the eggs with the cream and the fish liquor. Season and pour over the flan. Bake for about 45 minutes until the top is golden brown and the quiche is set in the centre.   SERVES 4–6.

MACKEREL LATTICE PIE

2 large mackerel (about 450 g/
    1 lb each), cleaned and
    filleted
25 g/1 oz butter
225 g/8 oz courgettes, sliced
100 g/4 oz mushrooms, sliced
1 × 400 g/14 oz can tomatoes
salt and freshly ground black
    pepper
½ teaspoon ground ginger
450 g/1 lb potatoes, cooked
    and mashed
1 egg, beaten
50 g/2 oz cheese, grated

Preheat the oven at 190°C/375°F/Gas Mark 5. Melt the butter in a pan and fry the courgettes and mushrooms for 2 minutes. Stir in the tomatoes, bring to the boil, season with salt, pepper and ginger. Pour half of the vegetables into an oven proof dish, lay the mackerel fillets on top and cover with the remaining vegetable mixture. Mix the mashed potato, cheese and egg together and pipe in a lattice over the dish. Bake for 20 minutes until golden brown.   SERVES 4.

KEBABS WITH SAVOURY RICE

3 rashers streaky bacon
1 plaice fillet (white skinned)
1 green pepper, deseeded and
    chopped
100 g/4 oz smoked oysters or
    mussels
12 button mushrooms
12 green grapes, halved and
    deseeded
2 tomatoes, cut into wedges
50 g/2 oz peeled prawns

SAVOURY RICE
75 g/3 oz rice
1 tablespoon salad oil
1 tablespoon vinegar
100 g/4 oz canned sweetcorn,
    drained
1 stick celery, trimmed and
    finely chopped
salt and freshly ground pepper

First prepare the *savoury rice*. Boil the rice until tender. Drain, mix with oil and vinegar and leave to cool. Add the sweetcorn and celery to the rice. Season to taste.

To prepare kebabs, grill bacon and cut into squares. Leave to cool. Poach plaice very carefully until just tender and leave to cool. Assemble the kebabs using small wooden skewers. Make up 12 kebabs with pieces of bacon, green pepper, smoked shellfish and button mushrooms. Make up a further 12 kebabs using halved grapes, pieces of plaice, tomato wedges and prawns. Arrange the kebabs on top of the savoury rice and serve with green salad.   SERVES 4–6.

STUFFED BAKED POTATOES

4 large potatoes
100 g/4 oz mushrooms, sliced
juice of 1 lemon
225 g/8 oz smoked haddock or
    cod
25 g/1 oz butter
salt and freshly ground pepper
50 g/2 oz grated cheese
1 tomato, sliced

Bake the potatoes in their jackets. Simmer the mushrooms in the lemon juice for 5 minutes. Drain and set aside. Poach the fish in a little water. When the fish is cooked, remove any skin and bones and flake. When the potatoes are cooked, cut in half and scoop out the pulp. Mash the pulp with butter. Add mushrooms and fish and season to taste. Stuff this mixture back into the empty potato jackets. Sprinkle with cheese and arrange a slice of tomato on top of each half. Finish off under the grill.

SERVES 4.

AUNTY MARY'S FISH HOT POT

750 g/1½ lb white fish fillets—
    hake, haddock or huss
stock to poach
4 onions, sliced
25 g/1 oz butter
4 potatoes
salt and freshly ground pepper
2 tablespoons single cream
25 g/1 oz grated cheese

Preheat the oven at 220°C/425°F/Gas Mark 7. Poach the fish in a little stock and cut into chunks. Fry the onions in butter. Boil potatoes in lightly-salted water and dice when cooked. Grease a casserole dish and layer potatoes, onions and fish, starting and ending with potatoes and sprinkling each layer with salt and pepper. Spoon on the cream and top with grated cheese. Bake for 10 minutes. If necessary, brown under the grill.

SERVES 4.

PARSLEY AND TARRAGON FISH CAKES

350 g/12 oz cooked white
    fish—huss, coley or pollack,
    flaked
450 g/1 lb cooked mashed
    potato
50 g/2 oz fresh breadcrumbs
3 tablespoons double cream
2 teaspoons anchovy essence
3 tablespoons chopped parsley
1 teaspoon dried tarragon
salt and freshly ground pepper
dried breadcrumbs to coat
oil for shallow frying

Mash the fish with a fork. Add the mashed potato, fresh breadcrumbs, cream, anchovy essence, herbs and seasonings. Beat to a smooth paste. Shape into flat cakes and coat with dried breadcrumbs. Fry in oil on each side until golden brown in colour.

SERVES 4.

Wholemeal Fish Crêpes

WHOLEMEAL FISH CRÊPES

*WHOLEMEAL
    PANCAKE BATTER*
225 g/8 oz wholemeal flour
½ teaspoon salt
4 eggs
4 tablespoons melted butter
250 ml/8 fl oz milk
250 ml/8 fl oz water
2 tablespoons oil

FILLING
25 g/1 oz margarine
1 carrot, diced
1 onion, diced
25 g/1 oz flour
280 ml/½ pint tomato juice
1 teaspoon dried oregano
*salt and freshly ground black
    pepper*
*450 g/1 lb huss or monkfish
    tails, boned and cubed*

First make the pancakes. Sift the flour and salt into a bowl. Make a well in the centre and add the eggs and melted butter. Gently fold into the flour with a wooden spoon and gradually add the milk and water until the mixture forms a smooth batter. Leave to stand for 2 hours.

Lightly grease a frying pan with a little of the oil and allow to get very hot. For each crêpe, pour in 4 tablespoons of batter and tilt the pan so the batter spreads to the edges. Cook for 1 minute then gently turn the crêpe and cook the other side for a further 30 seconds. Remove and keep warm and continue until the batter is all used.

For the filling, melt the margarine in a saucepan and fry the carrot and onion until just beginning to brown. Stir in the flour and cook, stirring for 2 minutes. Gradually add the tomato juice and heat, stirring until thickened. Stir in the herb, seasoning and cubed fish. Simmer for 10 minutes.

Fill the crêpes with the fish mixture and roll up. Serve hot.

SERVES 4.

QUICK MACKEREL CASSEROLE

425 g/15 oz canned mackerel, drained
300 g/10 oz canned condensed asparagus, tomato or mushroom soup
1 teaspoon dried marjoram
freshly ground black pepper
50 g/2 oz grated cheese
50 g/2 oz breadcrumbs

Preheat the oven at 200°C/400°F/Gas Mark 6. Flake the mackerel coarsely with a fork. Turn into a casserole dish and spoon the condensed soup over the top. Sprinkle with marjoram and black pepper. Mix the cheese and breadcrumbs and use to cover the dish. Bake for 40 minutes. If necessary brown the top under the grill. SERVES 4.

SPANISH WHITING

8 whiting fillets

STUFFING
1 small onion, finely chopped
grated rind and juice of 2 oranges
100 g/4 oz breadcrumbs
75 g/3 oz raisins
25 g/1 oz butter, melted
½ teaspoon dried mixed herbs
salt and freshly ground pepper

Preheat the oven at 190°C/375°F/Gas Mark 5. Mix the onion, orange rind, half the orange juice, breadcrumbs, raisins, melted butter, herbs and seasoning in a bowl. Spread this mixture over the fillets and roll up. Secure with cocktail sticks. Grease an ovenproof dish and place the fillets in it. Pour the remaining orange juice over the fish, cover and bake for 20 minutes. SERVES 4.

SCANDINAVIAN FISH PASTY

225 g/8 oz shortcrust pastry
225 g/8 oz cooked white fish—cod, haddock, coley or pollack, flaked
100 g/4 oz cooked rice
2 shallots or spring onions, finely chopped
2 large mushrooms, finely chopped
1 tablespoon chopped parsley
salt and freshly ground pepper
2 hard-boiled eggs, sliced

Preheat the oven at 200°C/400°F/Gas Mark 6. Roll out pastry into a 25 cm/10 in square. Mix the fish with the rice. Add the shallots, mushrooms and parsley. Season to taste. Place half the mixture in one half of the pastry. Arrange the eggs on top. Cover with remaining fish mixture. Fold the pastry over the top and seal. Make 3–4 slashes across the top of the pastry and place on a greased baking tray. Bake for 25–30 minutes until the pastry is lightly browned. SERVES 4.

GRILLED HALIBUT STEAKS WITH CHEESE TOPPING

4 × 275 g/10 oz halibut steaks
salt and freshly ground black
    pepper
50 g/2 oz butter, melted
1 onion, finely chopped
100 g/4 oz mushrooms, finely
    chopped
1 teaspoon dried tarragon
1 tablespoon lemon juice
100 g/4 oz cheddar cheese,
    grated

Remove the bone from the steaks if desired, season and place on a foil-lined grill pan. Brush with melted butter. Grill one side under a moderate grill for 4–5 minutes while preparing the topping.

Fry the vegetables in the remaining butter with the herb. Add the lemon juice and season to taste.

Turn over the halibut steaks and divide the topping between the steaks. Spread evenly. Top with grated cheese and replace under the grill for another 4 minutes. When cooked, serve hot with a crisp green salad.   SERVES 4.

Note The above topping may be used to top baked flat fish, or can even be used to stuff fillets. For whole fish, simply make 3 diagonal cuts across the prepared fish. Cover the fish with the topping, dot with a few knobs of butter and bake at 190°C/375°F/Gas Mark 5, for 20 minutes. Towards the end of cooking, cover with grated cheese and allow it to crisp up before serving.

MUSHROOM FISH PIE

450 g/1 lb potatoes
butter and milk to mash
salt and freshly ground pepper
350 g/12 oz white fish—cod,
    coley or haddock
200 g/7 oz canned tuna,
    drained
100 g/4 oz peeled prawns
100 g/4 oz mushrooms, sliced
300 g/10 oz canned condensed
    mushroom soup
juice of ½ lemon
25 g/1 oz grated cheese

Preheat oven at 190°C/375°F/Gas Mark 5. Boil the potatoes until cooked and mash with butter and milk. Season to taste. Poach the white fish in a little water until tender. Remove any bones or skin and flake. Flake the tuna. Mix white fish, tuna and prawns in a casserole dish. Place the mushrooms on top of the fish. Pour over the condensed soup and add lemon juice and seasoning. Cover with mashed potatoes and fork the top. Sprinkle with grated cheese and bake for 30–35 minutes until browned on top.   SERVES 4.

TAGLIATELLI WITH ANCHOVY PARMESAN SAUCE

225 g/8 oz tagliatelli
225 g/8 oz mushrooms, sliced
50 g/2 oz butter
2 teaspoons anchovy essence
300 ml/½ pint double cream
salt and freshly ground pepper
50 g/2 oz grated Parmesan
  cheese
4 canned anchovy fillets,
  drained and chopped

Cook the tagliatelli in lightly salted water until tender. Sauté the mushrooms in butter until tender. Drain the pasta and add the mushrooms and butter. Toss in the pan, add anchovy essence and double cream and season to taste. Serve sprinkled with Parmesan cheese and chopped anchovy fillets.   SERVES 4.

WINDSOR PIE

450 g/1 lb cooked white fish—
  haddock, hake, cod or
  coley, flaked
1 carton potted shrimps
100 g/4 oz mushrooms, sliced
25 g/1 oz butter
1 tablespoon cornflour
2 tablespoons sherry
150 ml/¼ pint fish stock and
  milk
salt and freshly ground pepper
100 g/4 oz shortcrust pastry

Preheat the oven at 220°C/425°F/Gas Mark 7. Grease a pie dish and place the fish in the base of it. Sprinkle with potted shrimps, retaining any large chunks of the shrimp butter. Sauté the mushrooms in butter and shrimp butter. Place mushrooms on top of the fish. Mix cornflour with sherry and pour into the pan the mushrooms have been cooked in. Add mixed fish stock and milk and bring to the boil, stirring all the time. Season to taste and pour over the fish. Roll out the pastry and top the pie with this. Fork the edges, prick the centre and bake for 20 minutes.   SERVES 4.

BULGARIAN FISH SUPPER

450 g/1 lb potatoes, chopped
2 onions, chopped
1 large green pepper, deseeded
  and coarsely chopped
4 tomatoes, skinned and
  coarsely chopped
4 tablespoons cooked rice
salt and freshly ground pepper
450 g/1 lb white fish—cod,
  coley or haddock

Preheat the oven at 190°C/375°F/Gas Mark 5. Mix all the vegetables together in a large casserole dish. Add the cooked rice and seasoning and mix again. Cover and bake for 30 minutes. Skin and bone the fish, if necessary, and cut into chunks. Stir into the casserole mixture. Replace the lid and continue cooking for a further 30 minutes.   SERVES 4.

GOLDEN GLOUCESTERSHIRE PIE

225 g/½ lb smoked cod fillet,
  skinned and cubed
225 g/½ lb coley fillet, skinned
  and cubed
280 ml/½ pint skimmed milk
25 g/1 oz margarine
25 g/1 oz flour
freshly ground black pepper
pinch nutmeg
50 g/2 oz button mushrooms,
  sliced
100 g/4 oz peeled prawns
350 g/¾ lb potatoes, scrubbed,
  sliced and cooked
50 g/2 oz low fat Cheddar
  cheese, grated

Preheat oven at 200°C/400°F/Gas Mark 6. Poach the fish in the milk for approximately 5 minutes. Drain, reserving 280 ml/½ pint liquid. To make the sauce, whisk together in a large saucepan the reserved liquid, margarine and flour over a gentle heat until thickened and smooth. Continue cooking for 2 minutes, stirring. Season with pepper and nutmeg and stir in the cubed fish, mushrooms and prawns. Put the mixture into an ovenproof dish and arrange the sliced potatoes over the filling. Sprinkle with grated cheese. Bake for 20 minutes until bubbling and golden.

SERVES 4.

Golden Gloucestershire Pie

77

SILVER BASS WITH CHEESE SAUCE

900 g/2 lb fresh silver bass fillets
50 g/2 oz butter or margarine
25 g/1 oz plain flour
¼ teaspoon garlic salt
freshly ground black pepper
275 ml/10 fl oz milk
100 ml/4 fl oz dry white wine
3 tablespoons grated Parmesan cheese
dash paprika

Preheat the oven at 180°C/350°F/Gas Mark 4. Cut the fish fillets into 6 serving-size pieces. Arrange the fish pieces in the bottom of a shallow baking dish. In a saucepan, melt the butter or margarine. Blend in the flour, garlic salt and season with pepper to taste. Add the milk and dry white wine slowly, stirring constantly and cook, stirring, until thickened and bubbly. Stir in 1 tablespoon of the grated cheese. Pour the sauce over the fish and bake for about 20–25 minutes, until the fish flakes easily when tested with a fork. Sprinkle the remaining cheese and paprika over the top and place under a grill until the cheese has just browned and the sauce is slightly bubbling, about 1 minute. Serve immediately.   SERVES 6.

SHRIMP JAMBALAYA

450 g/1 lb fresh shrimps or prawns
salt and freshly ground black pepper
1½ tablespoons butter
2 teaspoons flour
675 ml/24 fl oz chicken or fish stock
½ green pepper, finely chopped
3 spring onions, finely chopped
2 sticks celery, finely chopped
12 oysters
350 g/12 oz cooked ham, diced
225 g/8 oz cooked chicken, diced
450 g/1 lb cooked rice
fresh parsley, celery hearts, radishes and spring onions to garnish

First shell and clean the shrimp. Place in a saucepan, cover with cold water, season with salt and pepper and cook until tender, about 5 minutes. Drain and save the stock. In a large frying pan, melt the butter and stir in the flour. Slowly add the stock, stirring, and add the vegetables and oysters. Simmer until tender. Add the shrimp, ham, chicken and cooked rice. Stir until very hot. To serve turn the jambalaya out on to a hot plate and decorate with fresh parsley, celery hearts, radishes and spring onions.   SERVES 6.

NOODLES AMALFI

175 g/6 oz noodles
50 g/2 oz butter
50 g/2 oz flour
600 ml/1 pint milk
50 g/2 oz grated Parmesan
    cheese
salt and freshly ground pepper
450 g/1 lb peeled prawns
175 g/6 oz sliced mozzarella
    cheese

Preheat the oven at 200°C/400°F/Gas Mark 6. Cook the noodles in lightly salted water until just tender. Meanwhile melt butter in a pan and add the flour. Stir and gradually add the milk. Bring to the boil, stirring all the time, and add half the Parmesan cheese and season to taste. Drain the noodles and layer noodles, prawns, sauce, mozzarella and seasoning in a shallow earthenware dish ending with a layer of mozzarella. Sprinkle with remaining Parmesan and bake for 20 minutes.

SERVES 4.

GOLDEN GRILLED COD

4 cod steaks, about 2 cm/¾
    inch thick

TOPPING
50 g/2 oz mild Cheddar or
    Gruyère cheese
1 tablespoon margarine
2 tablespoons milk
salt and freshly ground pepper
grilled tomatoes and
    watercress to garnish

Trim and rinse the fish and pat dry. Place the fish in a greased shallow casserole and grill under moderate heat for 2–3 minutes on one side only. Meanwhile, grate the cheese and cream with the margarine. Beat in the milk, a few drops at a time, and season to taste.

Turn the fish over. Spread the topping on the uncooked side, and return to the grill. Reduce the heat slightly and cook for 10–12 minutes until the fish is cooked through and the topping is golden brown. Serve garnished with grilled halved tomatoes and watercress.

SERVES 4.

OYSTERS FLORENTINE

4 slices bread, crusts removed
oil for shallow frying
16 oysters, opened
100 g/4 oz frozen spinach
    purée, thawed
1 tablespoon double cream
cayenne to sprinkle

Fry the bread in cooking oil until golden on both sides. Drain, cut each into 2 and leave to cool. Heat the oysters through in a double steamer. Place spinach purée in a pan to thaw and heat through. Mix with cream and place a little of the mixture on each piece of fried bread. Place 2 warm oysters on each and press into the spinach. Sprinkle with cayenne and serve at once.

MAKES 8.

ANGELS ON HORSEBACK

12 small rashers streaky bacon
paprika
1 teaspoon chopped fresh
    parsley
lemon juice
12 oysters, opened
4 slices toast, cut into triangles

Season bacon rashers with paprika and sprinkle with parsley and lemon juice. Lay an oyster on each piece and roll up. Secure with a cocktail stick. Place under a hot grill until the bacon is crisp. Remove cocktail sticks and serve warm on toast.   MAKES 12.

CHEESE AND SARDINE FINGERS

125 g/4½ oz canned sardines in
    tomato sauce
4 slices toast, crusts removed
1 teaspoon chopped chervil or
    parsley
4 slices Cheddar cheese

Mash the contents of the can of sardines with a fork and spread over the toast. Sprinkle with chervil or parsley. Cut the slices of cheese to fit the toast and place on top. Place under a hot grill and cook until the cheese is brown and bubbling. Cut each slice into 3 fingers before serving. Serve hot.   MAKES 12.

PITTA PARCELS

2 large pitta breads
½ small savoy cabbage or crisp
    lettuce, finely shredded
3 medium carrots, finely
    shredded
6 spring onions, finely
    shredded
juice of ½ lemon
1 egg
2 teaspoons milk
200 g/8 oz flour
salt and freshly ground black
    pepper
200 g/8 oz fine dried
    breadcrumbs
3 tablespoons grated
    Parmesan cheese
½ teaspoon dried herbs—
    savory, chervil, chives, basil
    or tarragon
16 large peeled shrimp
50 g/2 oz butter
1 clove garlic, crushed

Cut the pitta bread in half lengthways and ease open carefully. Put aside. In a bowl mix together the shredded cabbage or lettuce, carrots and spring onions, sprinkle with the lemon juice and set aside. In a separate bowl beat together the egg and milk. Mix together the flour and seasoning, set aside and in another bowl mix together the breadcrumbs, grated cheese and dried herbs.

To fry the shrimp, first pat dry with kitchen paper. Dip each shrimp in the flour mixture and shake well to remove any excess flour. Then carefully dip each shrimp in the beaten egg making sure they are thoroughly coated. Then roll each shrimp in the breadcrumbs and again shake to remove any excess breadcrumbs. Set aside for 20 minutes.

Heat the butter in a heavy-based frying pan and fry the garlic gently. Add 3 or 4 shrimps at a time and fry, turning frequently to make sure all the sides become crisp and golden. Set aside on kitchen paper as you continue with the next batch.

Stuff each pitta half with the shredded vegetables and the fried shrimp and serve slightly warm.   SERVES 4.

Pitta Parcels

PARTY PIECES

Good enjoyable food is the making of a good enjoyable party. Whether it is a formal occasion, the food served on silver plates gently washed down with champagne, or a spontaneous gathering of friends, fish appetizers will always be popular.

For easy finger food try the pretty Assorted Pin Wheels (page 87) or the Smoked Haddock Profiteroles (page 86); their tasty lightness will surprise your guests! Or try something very different but so easy like the Prunes Stuffed with Mussels and Cream Cheese (page 84) or the traditional Greek Taramasalata (page 90); always a favourite served with Melba toast.

ANCHOVY AND OLIVE CANAPÉS

50 g/2 oz canned anchovy
  fillets, soaked and drained
12 stuffed olives
100 g/4 oz butter, softened
4 slices toast, crusts removed

Mince the anchovy fillets with 10 of the stuffed olives. Add the softened butter and spread the toast with this canapé mixture. Cut each toast in half to form two triangles. Thinly slice the remaining olives and use to decorate the canapés.

MAKES 8.

PIZZA FINGERS

225 g/8 oz self raising flour
1 teaspoon paprika
50 g/2 oz butter
1 egg
3 tablespoons milk

TOPPING
75 g/3 oz cream cheese,
  softened
6 tomatoes, skinned and sliced
1 small green pepper, sliced
1 × 225 g/8 oz 'hot' or 'cold'
  smoked mackerel fillet
watercress and lemon to
  garnish

Preheat the oven at 190°C/375°F/Gas Mark 5. For the base, sieve the flour and paprika into a bowl and rub in the butter. Beat the egg and milk together and add enough to the flour to make a soft dough. Knead lightly until smooth. Roll out into a 20 × 25 cm/8 × 10 in oblong and place on a greased baking sheet, spread the base with cream cheese, and lay the tomatoes and pepper on top. Skin and cut the mackerel into strips. Arrange on the pizza to form finger portions.

Bake for 30 minutes until the dough is risen and firm. Garnish with watercress and lemon. Cut into fingers to serve.

MAKES 8–10.

SMOKED SALMON CORNETS

225 g/8 oz smoked salmon

FILLING 1
2 eggs
15 g/½ oz butter
1 tablespoon milk
½ teaspoon dried tarragon
salt and freshly ground pepper

FILLING 2
1 portion Smoked Mackerel
  Paté (see page 86)
1 tablespoon double cream
parsley and lemon wedges to
  garnish

For the first filling, scramble the eggs with the butter and milk. Cook to a creamy consistency and remove from the heat. Do not overcook as the eggs will go hard and lumpy. Leave to cool and mix with tarragon and season to taste. For the second filling, mix one portion of the smoked mackerel pâté with cream to a smooth consistency. Cut the smoked salmon into 16 triangles and place a teaspoonful of egg filling in the centre of 8 of them and a teaspoonful of creamed pâté in the centre of the other 8. Roll up to make 16 cornets. Garnish with parsley and lemon wedges.

MAKES 16.

PRUNES STUFFED WITH MUSSELS AND CREAM CHEESE

*16 prunes, soaked in cold
    water overnight*
75 g/3 oz cream cheese
*1 tablespoon single cream or
    milk*
salt and freshly ground pepper
16 canned mussels

Bring the prunes to the boil in the water they were soaked in and simmer until just tender. Drain and leave to cool. Soften the cream cheese with single cream or milk and season to taste. When the prunes are cold, remove the stones and stuff with cream cheese and a single mussel. Serve with cocktail sticks. MAKES 16.

SMOKED GEMS

50 g/2 oz butter
50 g/2 oz flour
250 ml/8 fl oz milk
*100 g/4 oz smoked haddock or
    cod*
*175 g/6 oz Camembert or
    Brie, finely diced*
1 egg yolk
salt and freshly ground pepper
1 egg, beaten
dried breadcrumbs to coat
oil for deep frying

Melt the butter in a pan and add the flour. Stir well and gradually add the milk. Bring to the boil, stirring all the time. Continue cooking for 2–3 minutes and then remove from the heat. Poach the smoked haddock or cod in a little water. When cooked, drain, skin and flake the fish. Leave to cool. Mix the cheese into the sauce before it cools completely. Add the egg yolk and fork in the flaked fish. Season to taste. Place the mixture in the refrigerator for 2–3 hours. Shape the mixture into balls, dip in beaten egg and then roll in the breadcrumbs. Quickly deep fry in hot oil until golden. Do not leave in the hot fat for too long or the centres will begin to run. Drain and serve at once with cocktail sticks. MAKES 8–10.

SAMOSAS

FILLING
225 g/8 oz potatoes
100 g/4 oz huss
25 g/1 oz butter
1 tablespoon ground cumin
½ teaspoon ground ginger
½ teaspoon chilli powder
freshly ground black pepper
2 tablespoons frozen peas

PASTRY
100 g/4 oz flour
pinch salt
25 g/1 oz butter
2–3 tablespoons water
oil for deep frying

To make the filling, cook the potatoes in their skins in lightly salted water until tender. Steam the huss on a plate on top of the potatoes. Leave to cool and then peel and dice the potatoes and dice the fish. Melt the butter in a frying pan with the spices and sauté the potatoes, fish and peas in this until the potatoes and fish are lightly browned.

Meanwhile make the pastry by mixing the flour and salt and rubbing in the butter until the mixture resembles fine breadcrumbs. Bind with water and knead until the dough is firm and pliable. Roll the pastry out thinly and cut into 8 squares.

Place a little of the filling on each square and fold over in a triangular shape. Damp the edges and pinch together. Heat the oil and when it is really hot, fry the samosas until golden brown. Drain on kitchen paper and serve at once. MAKES 8.

Kipper Dip

KIPPER DIP

4 kipper fillets
50 g/2 oz softened butter
1 clove garlic, crushed
 (optional)
1–2 tablespoons single cream
140 ml/¼ pint mayonnaise
1 tablespoon lemon juice
salt and freshly ground black
 pepper
raw vegetables to serve (such
 as strips of cucumber,
 mushrooms, carrots, celery,
 red and green pepper and
 cauliflower florets)

Gently poach the kipper fillets in water for 5 minutes. Drain and chill. Remove the skin from the fillets and using a blender or food processor, flake the fish. Add the butter, garlic and single cream and blend well. Stir in the lemon juice and the mayonnaise and season to taste. Serve with raw vegetables.

SERVES 8–10.

SMOKED HADDOCK PROFITEROLES

CHOUX PASTRY
25 g/1 oz butter
150 ml/¼ pint water
50 g/2 oz flour
pinch of salt
1 egg
1 egg yolk

FILLING
100 g/4 oz smoked haddock
milk to poach
salt and freshly ground pepper
100 g/4 oz cream cheese

Preheat the oven at 200°C/400°F/Gas Mark 6. To make the choux pastry, heat the butter and water in a pan and when it boils remove from the heat. Stir in the flour and salt and mix well. Add the egg and egg yolk one at a time beating well between each addition. Spoon 16–20 small mounds on to a greased baking tray. Bake for about 20 minutes until the outside is golden brown and crisp and the inside is dry. Slit each profiterole and place on a wire rack to cool.

To make the filling, poach the haddock in a little seasoned milk. When it is cooked, remove from the cooking liquor, mash thoroughly with a fork and leave to cool. Mix with the cream cheese, adding a little of the cooking liquor if the mixture is too thick. Use to fill the profiteroles.   MAKES 16–20.

CHINESE SHRIMP TOAST

225 g/8 oz peeled shrimps or
*   prawns, finely minced*
6 spring onions, finely minced
1 small egg, beaten
½ teaspoon ground ginger
1 teaspoon sugar
1 tablespoon cornflour
salt and freshly ground pepper
4 slices bread, crusts removed
2 tablespoons sesame seeds
oil for shallow frying

Mix the shrimps or prawns and spring onions with the egg. Add ginger, sugar, cornflour and seasoning. Spread each slice of bread with the shrimp mixture and sprinkle with sesame seeds. Press these well into the top. Heat the cooking oil in a frying pan. Fry the slices of shrimp toast in oil, bread side down, until the bread turns golden brown. Turn over and fry the other side until it, too, turns golden brown. Remove from the fat and drain on kitchen paper. Cut into fingers and serve at once.   MAKES 12.

SMOKED MACKEREL PÂTÉ

100 g/4 oz butter
350 g/12 oz smoked mackerel
*   fillets, skinned*
juice of ½ lemon
75 g/3 oz cream or curd cheese
salt and freshly ground pepper
fresh parsley and lemon slices
*   to garnish*

Melt the butter in a saucepan. Place the mackerel, melted butter and lemon juice in a blender or food processor and blend until smooth. Add the cream cheese in small quantities and blend again. Season to taste and spoon into individual ramekin dishes. Place in the refrigerator to chill. Serve garnished with a little chopped parsley and very thin slices of lemon. Serve with fingers of brown toast.   SERVES 4–6.

MINIATURE CRAB QUICHES

PASTRY
40 g/1½ oz butter
40 g/1½ oz lard
175 g/6 oz plain flour
50 g/2 oz walnuts, ground
water to mix

FILLING
450 g/1 lb mixed crab meat,
    brown and white
75 ml/3 fl oz milk
2 eggs, beaten
225 g/8 oz cottage cheese with
    chives
pinch cayenne
2 teaspoons lemon juice
salt and freshly ground pepper

Preheat the oven at 200°C/400°F/Gas Mark 6. For the pastry, rub the butter and lard into the flour until the mixture resembles fine breadcrumbs. Stir in the walnuts and add sufficient water to mix to a soft dough. Roll out and use to line six individual quiche tins approximately 10 cm/4 in diameter.

For the filling mix together the remaining ingredients, season and divide mixture between the quiche tins. Bake for 35 minutes until golden brown. Cool slightly before removing from the tin. Serve hot or cold.   SERVES 6.

SMOKY CORN VOL-AU-VENTS

100 g/4 oz smoked cod
150 ml/¼ pint milk
½ green pepper, deseeded and
    finely chopped
15 g/½ oz butter
1 tablespoon flour
100 g/4 oz canned sweetcorn,
    drained
salt and freshly ground pepper
8 baked vol-au-vent cases

Poach the cod in the milk for 10 minutes. Blanch the pepper in boiling water for 8–10 minutes. Drain fish, retaining the liquid it was cooked in and drain peppers. Melt the butter in a pan and stir in the flour. Add the milk from the cod and bring to the boil, stirring. Continue cooking for 2–3 minutes, stirring all the time. Add flaked cod, pepper and the sweetcorn. Season to taste and warm through. Pile into warmed vol-au-vent cases. Serve warm.   MAKES 8.

ASSORTED PIN WHEELS

200 g/7 oz cream cheese
2 tablespoons single cream
1–2 teaspoons anchovy
    essence
salt and freshly ground pepper
25 g/1 oz minced smoked
    salmon
25 g/1 oz cod roe
6 slices fresh bread

Mix the cream cheese with the single cream to give a smooth creamy consistency. Divide the mixture in half and mix one half with anchovy essence and season to taste. Divide the remaining half again, mixing one part with minced smoked salmon and the other with cod roe. Season both to taste and add a little more cream if the mixtures seem to be too thick. Spread 2 slices of bread with each mixture. Remove the crusts and roll up lengthways. Slice into 5 pin wheels per slice.

MAKES 30.

CLAM DIP

225 g/8 oz cream cheese,
    softened
225 ml/8 fl oz soured cream
1 × 175 g/6 oz can clams,
    minced
1 tablespoon Worcestershire
    sauce
1 teaspoon grated onion

Mix together all the ingredients, place in a covered bowl and chill thoroughly. Serve with a variety of crisps and crackers.

SERVES 10–12.

HOT SEAFOOD DIP

2 × 225 g/8 oz packets cream
    cheese
4 tablespoons butter
50 ml/2 fl oz French
    vinaigrette dressing
1 × 200 g/7 oz can clams,
    minced, drained
1 × 200 g/7 oz can crab meat
⅛ teaspoon Worcestershire
    sauce
dash Tabasco
Melba toasts to serve

Blend together the cream cheese, butter and salad dressing. Add the minced clams, crab meat, Worcestershire and Tabasco sauce. Heat in a bain marie about half an hour before serving until piping hot. Serve with Melba toasts.

SERVES 10–12.

TAPENADE

18 anchovy fillets with oil
3 or 4 cloves garlic
50 ml/2 fl oz olive oil
20–24 black olives, stones
    removed
juice of ½ lemon
1 small can tuna with oil
50 ml/2 fl oz Cognac
raw vegetables to serve

In a blender or food processor put the first 3 ingredients and blend until smooth. Add the remaining ingredients and blend well. Place in a bowl and refrigerate until thoroughly chilled. Serve with raw vegetables.   MAKES ABOUT 225 ML/8 FL OZ.

SMOKED MACKEREL PITTA BREADS

450 g/1 lb 'hot' smoked
    mackerel fillets, skinned
    and diced
1 red pepper, deseeded and
    chopped
6 spring onions, chopped
3–4 leaves iceberg lettuce,
    shredded
chilli sauce to season
salt and freshly ground black
    pepper
4–6 pitta breads to serve

Mix the mackerel, pepper, onions and lettuce together.
Season to taste with chilli sauce and salt and pepper. Halve
the pitta breads, and carefully open up the cavities. Fill each
pitta bread with the smoked mackerel mixture and serve.

SERVES 4.

Smoked Mackerel Pitta Breads

TARAMASALATA

4 slices white bread
80 ml/3 fl oz milk
225 g/8 oz smoked cod roe
1 onion, chopped
150 ml/¼ pint olive oil
juice of 1 lemon
freshly ground black pepper
chopped parsley and chopped
   green olives to garnish

Soak the bread in the milk. Scoop out the roe from the skin and put into a blender or food processor. Add the onion, olive oil and lemon juice. Squeeze out the milk from the bread and add to the mixture, discarding the milk. Blend until smooth. Season with black pepper and garnish with parsley and green olives. Serve with Melba toasts.   SERVES 8–10.

EASTBOURNE PÂTÉ

350 g/12 oz haddock, skinned
150 ml/¼ pint milk and water
½ teaspoon dried tarragon
2 bay leaves
25 g/1 oz butter
25 g/1 oz flour
1 egg
salt and freshly ground pepper
thin slices cucumber to garnish

Poach the haddock in the milk and water with the tarragon and bay leaves. Remove the fish from the cooking liquor, discard the bay leaves and make the liquid up to 250 ml/8 fl oz with milk. Flake the fish and mash well with a fork. Keep on one side. Melt the butter in a pan and add the flour. Stir well and gradually add the milk and fish stock. Bring to the boil, stirring all the time, and cook for 2–3 minutes. Add the mashed fish, then the egg, and mix well. Season to taste. Grease a pudding basin and spoon the mixture into it. Cover with greaseproof paper and foil. Pour about 2.5 cm/1 in water into a large pan and place the basin in this. Bring the water to the boil and simmer for 45 minutes, topping up the water if necessary. Remove from the pan and leave to cool. Chill and turn out on to a serving dish. Garnish with thin slices of cucumber.   SERVES 4–6.

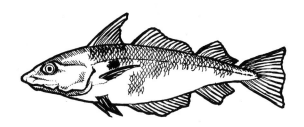

EGG AND MOCK CAVIAR COCKTAIL CUPS

12 small slices white bread
50 g/2 oz butter, softened
15 g/½ oz butter
2 tablespoons milk
3 eggs, beaten
salt and freshly ground pepper
1 × 50 g/2 oz jar lumpfish roe

Preheat the oven at 180°C/350°F/Gas Mark 4. Use a pastry cutter to cut bread into 12 rounds large enough to fit into deep bun trays. Butter both sides of each round with the softened butter and press into the cups of the bun tray. Bake for 25–30 minutes until golden brown. Remove from the tray and place on a wire rack to cool. Heat the butter and milk in a pan and add the eggs. Cook over a low heat, stirring all the time until scrambled. Do not allow the eggs to overcook. Season to taste and leave to cool. Fill the bread cups with cold scrambled egg and top with lumpfish roe.   MAKES 12.

CLARENCE CANAPÉS

4 slices bread
oil for deep frying
8–12 rashers streaky bacon
100 g/4 oz mushrooms, finely
    chopped
3 tablespoons anchovy essence
100 g/4 oz butter
1 slice cooked ham, finely
    chopped
chopped parsley to garnish

Cut each slice of bread into 2 or 3 fancy shapes with pastry cutters and deep fry in oil until golden brown. Drain and leave to cool. Grill the streaky bacon. Fry the mushrooms gently in a little cooking oil until they are soft; leave to cool. Cream together the anchovy essence and butter. Mix the ham with the mushrooms and bind with anchovy butter. Spread this mixture along the grilled bacon and roll up. Place each bacon roll on a piece of fried bread and garnish with chopped parsley.   MAKES 8–12.

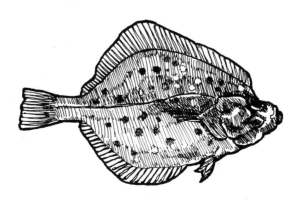

Duchy of Cornwall Pâté

DUCHY OF CORNWALL PÂTÉ

175 g/6 oz smoked cod roe,
   skinned
freshly ground black pepper
2 tablespoons fresh parsley,
   chopped
1 clove garlic, crushed
150 ml/¼ pint oil
2 tablespoons lemon juice
225 g/8 oz 'hot' smoked
   mackerel, skinned and
   boned
225 g/8 oz open mushrooms,
   cleaned and stalks reserved
croûtes of fried toast to serve

Place the roe, black pepper, parsley and garlic in a bowl and mix together well. Gradually beat in half the oil to make a good emulsion and stabilize by adding lemon juice and some boiling water slowly. Continue in this way with the rest of the oil. Mash the mackerel and blend with the roe mixture. Fill the cavities of the mushrooms with the pâté and garnish with the reserved mushrooms stalks. Serve on croûtes of fried toast.   SERVES 8–10.

SARDINE BITES

1 × 125 g/4½ oz can sardines
   in tomato sauce
75 g/3 oz cream cheese
salt and freshly ground pepper
6 slices buttered bread
2 eggs, beaten
oil for frying

Empty the contents of the can of sardines into a bowl and mash well with cream cheese until very smooth. Season to taste. Spread on to 3 slices of bread and sandwich with remaining slices. Cut off the crusts and cut each sandwich into 4 triangles. Dip each triangle in beaten egg and fry quickly on both sides in cooking oil. Serve at once.   MAKES 12.

FRIED SHRIMP

24 large raw shrimp, de-
  veined but leave the shells
oil for deep frying
8 cloves garlic
4 teaspoons salt

MARINADE
8 teaspoons grated fresh ginger
6 tablespoons rice wine

First prepare the marinade. Mix together the grated ginger and rice wine in a small bowl. Add the shrimp and marinate for about 30 minutes. Pat the shrimp dry with kitchen paper and deep fry them in the oil for 1 minute. Drain well. Just before serving, place the shrimp in a dry frying pan with the garlic and salt and stir-fry over a low heat until they are just heated through.   SERVES 4.

Fried Shrimp

TOASTED SARDINE ROLLS

12 skinless, boneless sardines
½ teaspoon Worcestershire
    sauce
½ teaspoon tomato ketchup
1 tablespoon finely-chopped
    onion
1 tablespoon finely-chopped
    stuffed olives
mayonnaise or French
    vinaigrette dressing to
    spread
salt and freshly ground black
    pepper
white bread, thinly sliced

Preheat the oven at 200°C/400°F/Gas Mark 6. In a bowl, mash the sardines together thoroughly with a fork. Add the Worcestershire sauce, ketchup, chopped onion and olives and mix together. Add enough mayonnaise or French dressing to the mixture to make a good spreading consistency. Season to taste with salt and pepper. Remove the crusts from the bread slices and spread with the sardine mixture. Roll the slices and secure with wooden cocktail sticks. Toast the rolls in the oven and serve immediately. MAKES 4–6.

SMOKED FISH SLICES

150 g/5 oz shortcrust pastry
225 g/8 oz smoked cod or
    haddock or kipper fillets
1 large onion, finely sliced
oil for frying
75 g/3 oz grated Cheddar
    cheese
3 eggs
150 ml/¼ pint milk
salt and freshly ground pepper

Preheat the oven at 190°C/375°F/Gas Mark 5. Roll out the pastry and use to line a 20 cm/8 in flan tin. Place the fish in a pan with a little water and poach for 8–10 minutes. Remove from the cooking liquid, flake and leave to cool. Fry the onion in cooking oil until transparent. Arrange the flaked fish and fried onion in the base of the flan and cover with cheese. Beat the eggs and milk together, season and pour into the flan. Bake for about 45 minutes until the top is golden brown and the quiche is set in the middle. Leave to cool for 20 minutes and then remove from the flan case and place on a wire rack until completely cold. To serve, slice into 6–8 pieces. SERVES 6–8.

MACKEREL PASTIES

450 g/1 lb shortcrust pastry
225 g/8 oz 'hot' smoked
   mackerel fillets
1 small onion, chopped
1 teaspoon lemon juice
1 tablespoon tomato ketchup
25 g/1 oz frozen peas
salt and freshly ground pepper
beaten egg to glaze

Preheat the oven at 200°C/400°F/Gas Mark 6. Roll out the pastry into an oblong measuring 24 × 36 cm/9 × 14 in and cut into 6 squares.

Remove the skin and any bones from the mackerel, flake and mix in a bowl with remaining ingredients. Place a spoonful of mixture on to each pastry square. Dampen the edges and fold over to form a triangle. Seal well.

Place on a baking sheet and brush with the beaten egg. Bake for 30 minutes until golden brown. Serve hot or cold with a crisp salad.

SERVES 6.

SMOKED SALMON AND EGG TARTS

175 g/6 oz shortcrust pastry
50 g/2 oz frozen peas
sprigs of watercress to garnish

FILLING
4 eggs, beaten
2 tablespoons milk
butter to scramble
100 g/4 oz smoked salmon,
   diced
salt and freshly ground pepper

Preheat the oven at 200°C/400°F/Gas Mark 6. Roll out the pastry and use to line 12 tartlet tins. Prick the bases with a fork. Fill with foil and dry beans and bake blind for about 10 minutes. Remove the foil and beans and continue cooking until golden in colour. Remove from the tins and place on a wire rack to cool. Cook the peas as directed on the packet.

To make filling, scramble the eggs with the milk and knob of butter until soft and creamy. Remove from the heat and leave to cool in the pan, stirring from time to time. Take care not to overcook the eggs. Mix the smoked salmon with the cold scrambled eggs and season to taste. Spoon the mixture into the tartlets and decorate with cold peas. Serve garnished with watercress.

MAKES 12.

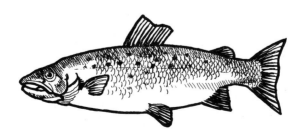

INDEX